Asyniur
Womens Mysteries in the Northern Tradition

Sheena McGrath

Asyniur
Womens Mysteries in the Northern Tradition

©1997 Sheena McGrath

ISBN 1 86163 004 2

ALL RIGHTS RESERVED

Cover design by Paul Mason

Published by:

Capall Bann Publishing
Freshfields
Chieveley
Berks
RG20 8TF

Contents

Introduction

This book is intended to be an introduction to the Norse goddesses and heroines, along with the women who believed in them. In it I will describe the various goddesses, the main myths, and their ideas about the cosmos. I will also discuss my ideas about Norse myth, which are shaped mostly by my feminism and what I read of other people's ideas on the subject.

My interest in Germanic mythology began early. At about age ten, I was reading a book on Greek myths, and at the back was a section on the Norse myths. This retelling of the Eddas for children concentrated on comparing the Norse with the Greeks, rather to the Norse's detriment. For some reason, this made me feel for those northern gods, and their (apparently inferior) goddesses.

Time passes, and the Eddas have become respectable myths in their own right. While it is unlikely that the volume of books on Norse myth will ever match that of the Greeks, anyone so foolhardy as to ask for all the books on the Norse deities available had better be as mighty as Thor to carry them home. The goddesses, however, remain obscure.

Frigg and Freya get some coverage, especially from male writers who see them as the two halves of the archetypal female (wife and lover). The other goddesses get passed over unless they can be shown to be sexually involved with an important god. The sun-goddess is continually ignored in favour of Odin, Thor, Heimdall, or Baldr, despite the fact that the sources we have say that there is a female sun. (See the Gender and Mythology chapter for more on this.)

Sexism is apparent in the assumptions that are made about the nature of the goddesses. It is often assumed that all of them are one goddess; no one, however, suggests that the gods might all be aspects of Odin. The trick here is to first not give much information about the various goddesses and then state that their lack of differentiation means that they are all basically the same.

Another typical manoeuvre is to imply that they are basically fertility figures, and thus not as interesting as the gods of civilisation. Obviously the idea that nature is feminine and culture masculine has been at work here, so that the writer concludes that the goddesses have nothing to do with the work of sophisticated urban civilisations. It also says that whatever women do is less significant that what men do.

In short, the goddesses aren't as important as the gods to many writers. Even minor or confusing gods get whole books by scholars like Georges Dumézil, but few writers have considered why Gefjon is a virgin in some myths and not in others. Now that women are working at universities in large numbers, this is beginning to change. I was delighted to find articles considering how much sexist ideas about women informed the notions about the goddesses. Writers like Lotte Motz and Margaret Clunies Ross are analysing the myths from a feminist perspective and coming up with some very interesting ideas.

What's in it for women?

Women are changing the face of the Northern mysteries outside of the universities as well:

"On its founding day the 'Hof membership was one hundred percent male, which continued for a while. Now the figure is split one third women and two thirds men." This quote comes from Martyn H. Taylor in the fourteenth issue of *Odalstone*, the Odinshof journal. This neo-pagan organisation has been around for ten years, during which time more and more women have become interested in the Northern Tradition. There are still many people who find this interest odd, or even see it as flying in the face of all women's gains in the past thirty years.

Surely women are as likely to change the structures of Asatru and the other groups as much as they have the business world. The assumption that these groups and the women in them are right-wing and therefore uninterested in feminism does not hold. The independence that the Northern tradition encourages makes its followers sceptical and unlikely to bow to authority, as well as making life a lot easier for powerful women.

Besides, it ignores the real issue of why women are interested in these groups. I suspect that it has to do with the rise of the image of the powerful, competent woman in the media. Women want to see themselves as victors, not victims. The Norse and German myths definitely fill that need, with their many heroic women. In some myths Frigg shows a cunning equal to Odin's, and so wins out over him, while she and Freya use magic to support their worshippers successfully.

There is definitely a perception that the Germans and Norse were extremely sexist warriors who had little time for or interest in women. If that was actually true, I wouldn't have written this book, nor would women be joining groups like the Odinshof, Ring of Troth, and many others. When you consider that the common image of the Nordic woman is that of a Valkyrie, you have to admit that, in perception at least, Norse women were not not wimps. Reality, while less dramatic, bears this out: women were sometimes warriors, ran farms and businesses, and could get a divorce simply and without any single-mother stigma. Compare this to the Classical culture of Athens, where women had to stay in their quarters, and men even did the shopping, so that women wouldn't be out on the streets.

For the less warlike among us, it is reassuring to know that the Germanic peoples (which includes the Norse, who were German colonists) were not all warriors. While most of the population would fight in a war, especially if their homes were threatened, the most common activities were farming and trading. However, it is interesting that warrior cultures like Sparta, Ireland and Germany seemed to provide a better deal for women than more peaceful ones nearby.

That feminists within the women's spirituality movement continue to be obsessed with Greek mythology and religion is strange, considering what a sexist society ancient Greece was. By comparison, the Germanic goddesses are strong, relatively autonomous figures, and the women who worshipped them certainly had more rights.

Of course, these attractions are often unreasonable, having more to do with which pantheons resonate with our psyches than any practical considerations. All the same, it seems to me masochistic to actively seek out and work with the pantheons most oppressive to women.

Religious History

Heathendom is, that men worship idols; that is, they worship heathen gods, and the sun or moon...[1]

The Germans are usually divided into three groups. The West Germans include the English, Germans, and Dutch. The North Germanic peoples include the Danes, Swedes, Icelanders and Norwegians. The East Germans are an extinct population, but the Goths were once important, providing many of our early texts in the Germanic language family.[2] Unfortunately, there are no consistent records for any group. Historians have had to piece together information from archaeology, Roman writings, and the later records of the Germans and especially Scandinavians.

This chapter will try to trace the history of paganism among these peoples from the first Germans to the triumph of Christianity. It will be slightly biased in favour of women's activities and female deities, since these tend to be overlooked in orthodox histories. Readers will notice that I am assuming that the religious practices and beliefs of the various Germanic people didn't change all that much.

In fact, it is difficult on balance to say how much they did change, or when. While some deities and practices don't seem to have changed at all (sacrifices) others seem to have vanished (twin gods) or become much less important (the solar cult). In the rest of the book I focus on the

Norse and their written sources, so the history is biased towards finding patterns of continuing practices and beliefs.

Bronze Age

The oldest community of Germanic people was the Jastorf culture. This settlement dates from about the 6th century BCE. They lived the areas of Holstein, north-west Low Saxony, the major part of the Altmark and West-Mecklenburg. From there they spread into Jutland, western Pomerania, and the Elster, Mulde and Saale area. The Jastrof culture was a stable one. They seem to have been nomadic hunters who followed their food, but found this area so congenial they stayed there. No doubt they had a major impact on the farmers living there before their arrival. However, once the local population assimilated them, there is little change through the Bronze and Iron Ages. A nearby culture was the Harpstead, who occupied an area to the west of the Jastrof. These two cultures are generally agreed to be the original Germans.

Our main source of information about Bronze Age religion is the art found in graves and carved on rocks. The common custom among the Germans was to burn the dead on a pyre, and then bury the remains in an urn, along with some goods for use in the afterworld. In the Bronze Age weapons were a favourite burial item, as well as ornaments. Funeral mounds are rare at this time. The dead person's possessions were often broken, which archaeologists think would magically render them useless in this life, but useful in the next.

Another source of information on Bronze Age religion is the drawings inscribed on cliffs in Scandinavia and the lower Baltic shore. Some of these go back to 1500 BCE, and the more frequent motifs give some idea of religious beliefs back then. These themes include: weapons, twin figures, animals, ships, hands, feet, long-haired figures in robes, and discs.

The weapons and people bearing them are probably Odin, Tyr and Thor. The gods are usually associated with particular weapons, which is how the carvings were identified. The spear was Odin's weapon, often thrown over the heads of an enemy warband to dedicate them to the god. (Thus killing the enemy became an offering to Odin, a human sacrifice.) Tyr was generally associated with the sword. Thor is of course the god of the hammer, but in Bronze Age art the thunder-god carried an axe. The hammer was an Iron Age technology.

Another set of symbols that commonly appears on the rocks is the twins. These two figures are pictures on ships, or holding axes. These are often associated with the Heavenly Twins of Indo-European myth, such as Castor and Pollux of the Romans. Finding these twins in later myth is something of a problem, with candidates ranging from Baldr and Freyr to the Alcis described by Tacitus but otherwise invisible.

Figures of long-haired people in dresses are generally taken to be women, which suggests goddesses or priestesses. These women are also often depicted aboard ships, with other figures or else alone. None of these women carry weapons, nor do they have any attributes or make any gestures. By contrast, other figures stand with upraised arms, their legs wide apart, and a cup-mark (a round indentation in the rock) between their legs.[3] These could be seen as an equivalent to the many figures of men with enormous penises, since the indented marks probably indicate the women's vulvas. The figures' raised hands are probably indicators of priestly blessing, as this is the usual explanation for the male figures. If they are goddesses, they are probably Vanir, since those deities were closely tied to the sea and sexuality as well as fertility.

Many of the scenes of women with other figures have been interpreted as "sacred marriages", a wedding of either two deities or a deity and a human. Often they showed a couple embracing, on a ship or on land. In one a large figure raised an axe over a male and female pair. (Thor's axe/hammer was used to bless holy occasions such as marriages - like in the Eddic poem *Thrymskvida*.)

These pictures are often assumed to be an earth- sky mating, which fertilises the earth. Lotte Motz, however, suggests that the plethora of male figures with erect penises are more likely fertility symbols, just as in the Eddic creation myths the worlds are made by men. She believes that the concept of Father Sky marrying Mother Earth and making her fruitful is a modern myth.[4] (See the chapter Gender and Mythology for more on fertility gods.)

The disc was one of the most common figures in the rock carvings. It probably represented the sun, an interpretation borne out by the figures of two horses pulling a disc in a chariot. The sun-disc was also pictured mounted on a ship, which represented the journey of the sun at night, across the water to the east. However, the gender of the sun in these pictures is open to question. Some read the little men (if one interprets the little "tails" that end their bodies as penises) who held sun-discs like shields and the disc-with-axe motif as images of a sun-god. There are other explanations, however. The sun and axe could represent a mating scene, since the axe represents the thunder-god. The sun is a feminine presence across

Northern Europe, in both Indo- European and other cultures, so the sun-god explanation seems unlikely.

Hands and feet were also popular symbols. The sun-disc sometimes had hands or feet. The hands would probably have been a symbol of blessing, like the gestures of the priestess/goddess figures discussed above. The feet may be connected to a later tradition which held that the sun danced on Easter morning, leaving its footprints on rocks. The footprints on their own are interpreted as fertility symbols. (They may be related to the myth of Skadhi's marriage, when she chooses her groom by looking at his bare feet.)

Another source of information about the Bronze Age religion is the art of the period. It is here that we have our best source of information about the goddesses of the time. One well-known figure shows a woman kneeling up as if to ride a chariot. She has large, protruding eyes and wears a miniskirt of cords tied at the waist and hem. She raises one hand, perhaps for the reins, while the other cups a breast. A snake found in the same place was probably her mount. Other figures carry bowls, kneel with their hands on their breasts, or bend backwards so their heads touch the ground.[5] Along with the female statues, small axe-men were found at Grevens Vaeng. These may represent Thor, the Heavenly Twins or else Odin's son Forseti, a god of justice who carried a single-bladed axe like the figures'.

Another important find was the Trudholm chariot, which is a model of a six-wheeled chariot carrying a disc, pulled by a horse (which rests on four wheels). This corresponds to the many figures of discs and discs in chariots found in the rock carvings. The solar cult probably involved rolling this in imitation of the sun's course through the sky.

The Roman Period

Obviously all theories about the petroglyphs and other items from the Bronze Age are guesses - there are no signs or labels to tell us what their makers intended them to mean. The first written information about Germanic religion comes from the encounter between the Germans and the Roman army, in the first century CE. While these are unlikely to be unbiased sources, they are all we have for this period.

Julius Caesar wrote at length about the Germans in his *De Bello Gallico*. He didn't conquer them, but he learned what he could. Another Roman, Tacitus, wrote about the Germans in the same way that some Europeans later wrote about the Native Americans. He contrasted their simplicity and morality with the decadence of Roman life, and used them for propaganda purposes to fulminate against his fellow citizens.

Julius Caesar stated that the Germans worshipped the sun, moon and Vulcanus, which was a Latin way of saying fire. He probably found that the Germans had a lunar calendar, and guarded their hearth-fire in the usual Indo-European way. Seeing this, he may have concluded that they worshipped the moon and fire. The Romans also dated religious festivals by the lunar months, and reverenced the hearth in the form of Vesta, an old and important goddess. It seems that the sun-deity was more important to the Germans than the Romans, who didn't really get excited about solar worship until later. Some people see "Vulcanus" as a Roman interpretation of Wayland/Volund the magical smith, and either reading is possible.

Just to make things more confusing, Tacitus mentions another set of gods.

> *Above all other gods they worship Mercury, and count it no sin, on certain feast-days, to include human victims in the sacrifices offered to him. Hercules and Mars they appease by offerings of animals, in accordance with civilised custom. Some of the Suebi sacrifice also to Isis.*[6]

(The Suebi was a generic name for Germans of the north and east.) Tacitus, of course, calls his deities by Roman names, but they are generally thought to be Odin, Thor and Tyr. The goddess represented by Isis is more mysterious. This could be Nerthus, whose temple was near the sea, or the Dutch goddess Nehallenia, the protector of sailors. (She, like Isis, had a ship as an attribute.)

As Tacitus implies, sacrifice was important to the Germans, as a way of making a bond between them and the gods. They threw food, often gruel in clay bowls, into bogs. They also put weapons in the bogs, as well as costly items like the Gundestrup Cauldron and the Trudholm Chariot mentioned earlier.[7] Horses, cattle and dogs have also been found, although only certain bones from the cattle were there, so perhaps the celebrants ate some of the cow first. Dogs were also laid into graves. Later, flax bundles and butter became common offerings, and small drinking vessels. (The flax and food suggest that women made some of the offerings, perhaps as part of the cult of the goddesses.)

There was some human sacrifice, although there is controversy over how many of the women found dead in bogs were killed for various crimes and how many were actual gifts to the gods. (Sometimes these two categories overlapped.) In one case, a girl's body was found at Windeby in Domland Fen, one side of her head shaved, blindfolded, wearing an ox-hide collar around her neck and nothing else.[8] Tacitus' description of the punishment for adultery - the wife's head was shaved and she was stripped and flogged out of town - indicates that the woman in the bog may have been punished this way.

Tacitus is our one source for the details of the worship of a goddess called Nerthus, and the Alcis. Of this goddess he says:

> They believe she takes part in human affairs, riding a chariot among her people. On an island of the sea stands an inviolate grove, in which, veiled with a cloth, is a chariot that none but the priest may touch. The priest can feel the presence of the goddess in this holy of holies, and attends her with deepest reverence as her chariot is drawn along by cows. Then follow days of rejoicing and merrymaking in every place that she condescends to visit and sojourn in. No one goes to war, no one takes up arms; every iron object is locked away. Then, and then only, are peace and quiet known and welcomed, until the goddess, when she has had enough of the society of men, is restored to her sacred precinct by the priest. After that, the chariot, the vestments, and (believe it if you will) the goddess herself, are cleansed in a secluded lake. This service is performed by slaves who are immediately afterwards drowned in the lake.[9]

In the same rather sceptical vein, he describes the cult of the Alcis as run by transvestite priests who worshipped gods he calls Castor and Pollux, the Roman Heavenly Twins. No images were ever made of these deities.

Tacitus also says that women were important religious figures to the Germans. While they didn't see them as goddesses (an important point, since this might imply

12

that they were put on a pedestal, an old trick), they respected women's prophetic abilities. He mentioned a woman called Veleda, whom many Germans considered a divinity, and another called Aurinia.

This Veleda was prominent in the Batavi's revolt against Civilis (69-70 CE). Other famous prophetesses included a woman of the Chatti who advised Emperor Vitellus, and Baulburg, named on a pottery fragment from Elephantine in the second century CE.[10]. Caesar backs this up, saying that a German general would not fight because "matrons" had drawn lots and decided the Germans would lose if they fought before the new moon.[11]

The Goths

The Gothic people migrated from southern Scandinavia into the Black Sea area. They conquered the people there, and later moved into Dacia, and their empire at its greatest spanned the Ukraine and reached from Belarus to the Black Sea. The Huns defeated them in 370 CE, which pushed them into Italy and the Roman Empire into collapse. They held Italy and Spain for awhile, losing out to the Franks and others later.

One of the most notable things about the Goths is that they were Christians by the time they reached Italy. However, they were the "wrong kind" - Arians, who believed with Arianus that Jesus was a sort of demi-god. (Official Catholic doctrine holds that Jesus is both god and man, at once.[12]) This did not make them very popular with other Christians, who were engaged in eliminating the Arian heresy. The fact that the Arians had sent missions to the heathens was causing the orthodox Christians some problems.

Unfortunately, the main mass of texts in Gothic was burned in a bonfire intended to destroy all heretic texts, so much of the information on the Goths was lost. The Eastern Roman Empire defeated them during its campaign to take back Rome, and the Moors took over their Spanish possessions. This loss of political power makes it difficult to trace the movements of the Goths. Eventually their language died out as well, and was last spoken in the Crimea during the sixteenth century.

The Anglo-Saxons

Another Germanic expansion led the Saxons Hengst and Horsa to England circa 525 CE. Naturally the Saxons brought their pagan beliefs with them. The British Isles were at that time populated by the Celts, who had been resisting the Germanic incursions for about 100 years. The collapse of the Celtic resistance at this time allowed the Germans to move in and build up the new Anglo-Saxon culture.

Naturally, the church sent out missionaries to these new heathens in the hope of converting them. They arrived at the end of the century, and the balance of power see-sawed between the pagans and Christians for the next two hundred years. (The Goths had already been converted, and participated in the Council of Nicea in 325 CE.) There were some interesting outbreaks of paganism, and at least one king had a shrine with altars to both the pagan gods and Christ.

The testimony of churchmen and kings who tried to legislate Christian behaviour is all we have concerning these people. However, the laws against pagan behaviour give some idea of what was being forbidden. Canute, for example, forbade worship of the sun, moon, and fire, as well as groves and streams. (Clearly he hadn't heard that Julius Caesar is considered wrong by modern scholars.[13])

The Venerable Bede (673-735 CE) gives us the calendar in use by the pagans, along with the names of two goddesses otherwise unknown, Hretha and Eostre. He says that the pagan year began on Dec. 25th. The next night was Modra necht, "mothers night", although he doesn't say anything about the festival. The next major festival was in the second month, Solmonath. This was when people offered cakes to the gods. This was probably a modified form of the festivities that surround St. Bride's Day, since Sól was the Norse sun-goddess. The harvest festival was in the month called Halegmonath, "Holy month", and the last month of the year was Blotmonath, from the Norse word *blot*, a sacrifice. (This corresponds to the Celtic Samhain and All Hallows Day.)

The Anglo-Saxons kept up the old worship, building temples and images of their deities. Odin, Tiw and Thor were certainly revered, as well as the goddess Frig. Many place-names record their presence, The Domesday Book mentions the Frigefolc, which could be translated "Frig's People". In Hampshire, her name appears in Fryole and Frobury. Apparently both once were Freohyll, "Frig's Hill". Others include Fryup in the North Riding, and Frydaythorpe in the East Riding. Magic was also part of English paganism. A few women's tombs contained strainers, crystal balls and tweezers hung from the women's belts, which may have been used in divination.[14] The role of women as diviners had not changed from the period of Roman contact.

The Vikings

While women's magical practices remained much the same, the world was changing around them. Economic pressures were forcing men to take up raiding and colonising other areas. Women frequently accompanied their men on these voyages, sometimes as warriors, but more often as settlers. They kept up their religious functions in these new lands; a woman called Ota prophesied from the altar of Clonmacnoise in Ireland, after the church was ransacked by the warriors. She must have been a seeress of some kind, and this confirms that women gave advice to warriors. Other women accompanied them as warriors, and their stories appear in the chapter on Women in Norse Society.

The goddesses appear to have gone underground during this period. We know from Christian baptism oaths that the main German gods of this period were Odin, Thor and Saxnot (a personification of the sword). The pagans still took the honour of their gods seriously. A Christian convert insulted Freya at the 999 CE Althing in Iceland; for calling her a bitch, he was exiled. He barely escaped more physical punishment by some of the others present.[15] In response to the crosses sported by the converts, the pagans began wearing Thor's hammers, often with his face carved into the head of the hammer's handle.

The temples and priesthood reached their apex during this period. The Germans, like the Celts, had originally carried out their worship outdoors, in groves or near springs or waterfalls. Later they began using hogr, which means "cairn" and was probably a heap of stones that sacrifices were offered on. Sometimes altars or images enclosed in tents were also called hogr .

In one poem Ottar makes such offerings to Freya, who then helps him. Many hogr were raised to the disir and other goddesses. We know from vocabulary that libations and sacrifice were part of religion. Animals were offered to the gods and eaten by the celebrants, while their blood was sprinkled about as a gift to the gods.

By the ninth century, elaborate wooden enclosures appeared, housing statues of the deities as well as the sacred apparatus. The temple of Odin, Thor and Freyr at Uppsala in Sweden is one famous example. These buildings were called hofs, and functioned as a private or public temple, run by the priest(ess). The priest(ess) could appear in very fine clothes and jewels, as well as possessing an oath-ring of precious metal. In Iceland the priests were called godi, and priestesses gydia. They had civil authority as well as being religious officials, and the title was hereditary. (Women had to cede the civil authority, but apparently could have the temple office.[16])

Some interesting graves from this period show that the practice of sacrificing servants when the master died was a non- discriminatory one. At Dråby in Denmark, a housewife was buried along with a male who had been decapitated, and in Gerdup a woman was buried with a man whose hands and feet had been bound, and his neck broken.[17] However, human sacrifice doesn't seem to have been a common thing. The likelihood of a wife being sacrificed when her husband died appears to have been small. Female and male slaves might not be so lucky, at least among the Rus, who had moved to Kiev. One Arab writer (Ibn Fadlan) says that a female slave would volunteer to die with her master, and so was cremated with him.

Christianity and the Icelandic Resistance

This really was the last of pagan culture. Iceland decided in 1000 CE to have everyone baptised, so that the sort of strife stirred up by insults to Freya and other deities would stop. Charlemagne had conquered the Franks long before, and Canute had put down a revival of paganism in England. Norway was a dual-faith area for awhile, but the king who became St. Olaf forced his people into orthodoxy by the new millennium. Sweden held out longest, until 1100.

Of course, all these areas had lasting pockets of paganism that held out against all efforts to Christianise them. Iceland really had been the last stronghold where pagans could live in peace, because there was no king to compel them to convert.

Pagan practices were still permitted in Iceland after 1000 CE, despite the conversion to Christianity. The Family Sagas also show a conflict between the pagan and Christian elements of society. There was also an attempt to match the Christians in religion. Temples became richer, with ornamented statues and large offerings.

The pagans sometimes managed to de-convert people, or at least express their disapproval of the newly Christian. King Haakon of Norway was compelled to drink toasts and eat horse liver at a sacrifice by his followers, in violation of his new religion. Despite the resistance, however, Christianity spread among the upper classes, and from there into the peasantry.

We get most of our written sources on Norse myth and legend from medieval Scandinavia. *The Eddas*, Saxo Grammaticus' history of Denmark, and the sagas provide the information on belief and practice. They are also quite obviously written by people who don't believe everything in the stories, especially the *Prose Edda*, which was written much later than the others.

The *Eddas* were written down in Iceland, and reflect the myths and history of that land. The idea of the world being born of ice and fire makes sense in a land racked by volcanoes and positioned in the far north. In the *Prose Edda*, Snorri Sturluson sets out the basics of Norse myth, although argument rages over how much he made up. He contrives to mention most of the legends connected to the major deities, at least in outline.

There are some oddities, especially in his treatment of the goddesses. He mentions several goddesses unknown outside his text and, confusingly, tells the story of how Gefjon used sex to obtain Zealand, but then calls her a maiden, patron of virgins. It could be said that he created as many mysteries as he resolved.

Saxo Grammaticus does not seem to like the Norse deities very much. He also presents them as humans whose fame made them gods, but his view is that they were rather immoral humans. He also pokes fun at scholars who Romanised the pantheon, by pointing out the tangled family relations that result. His attitude to the goddesses is that they are as tricky as the gods, and lascivious as well. His presentation of Frigg, Freya and Gefjon shows them as greedy, oversexed, and overshadowed by the gods.

This final denigration of the Norse deities marked the triumph of Christianity. From then until the revival of paganism in modern times, the gods and goddesses were underground, worshipped in secret if at all. However, nationalism brought them into the fore again, as Jacob

Grimm tried to prove that the Germans had a culture which owed nothing to the Graeco-Roman tradition. This was another turning-point, and from then on the deities began to come into the light again.

Origins

Snorri Sturluson's *Edda* (sometimes called the *Prose* or *Younger Edda* to distinguish it from the *Poetic* or *Elder Edda* he uses as source material) synthesises earlier poets into a coherent account of Norse poetry and myth. It is from the two *Eddas* that we have the story of the world's origin. In the beginning was the fire in the south, and the ice in the north. In the gap between them the giant Ymir was formed. The first frost-giants were formed from his sweat.

A cow called Audhumla had also come into being, and she licked the ice until a man called Buri was born. This man eventually had a son called Bor (from where we don't know) who married a woman called Bestla (a giant's daughter). Their children were the god Odin and his two brothers, Villi and Vé (Will and Holiness).

The three brothers killed Ymir, and made the nine worlds from his body. Ymir's skull became the sky, his bones the earth, and his blood the sea that surrounded the earth. Bor had four dwarves as sons, and the gods set the sky on their shoulders, stationing one at each cardinal point. After this they made the first humans, from trees. The man Ask was formed from an ash tree, and Embla was made from an alder or elm. Then Odin gave them breath and life, Hoenir gave them senses, and Loddur gave them redness of face or vitality. (In this creation myth, Odin's two brothers were Hoenir and Loddur, rather than Vili and Vé.) This creation myth was a very masculine one, which required very little female input.

The existence of classes was explained by another myth, which was an origin story for society. A god named Rigr came to Midgard, and stayed a night with a human couple. That night Rigr lay with the woman, Edda (Great-grandmother). After he left she gave birth to the first of the thralls (slaves). Then Rigr lay with another human woman, Amma (Grandmother), and so she was the mother of the churls (freemen). His last lover was Mothir (Mother), the ancestress of the jarls (aristocrats).

This Icelandic myth, which presupposes some female involvement, is different from the story Tacitus got from the Germans. He says that the first human was the bisexual Tvisto, who gave birth to three sons, Ingvio, Irmio and Istio. (The names are suggestive of Ingve-Freyr and the Irminsul pillar which stood for Tyr and Yggdrasil.) These three were the ancestors of the Ingaevones, Herminones, and Istaevones, three German tribes. Once again we find the idea of a purely male creation, in contrast with the more orthodox births of the three classes.

The male appropriation of the female role of giving birth and nurturing is significant, because when Norse men or gods took on female roles, they usually incurred the penalty of ergi, effeminacy. While this may not be so serious to us, to the ancient Norsemen this was a deadly insult. But in the creation myth the gods and giants give birth and nurture their creation, without any stain of femininity. This may be a backhanded tribute to the perception of women's ability to give birth as supremely powerful, so powerful that a man who took on this power was not scorned for it.

However, as Margaret Clunies Ross points out, most societies that endorse the male "birthing" do so in the belief that the second birth of a man into society by male agency is much more important than the original birth from the mother.[18] This would explain the lack of women in the origin myths, a lack so noticeable that in the *Gylfaginning* King Gylfi asked the Æsir:

> "*How did generations grow from him, and how did it come about that other people came into being, or do you believe him to be a god who you have just spoken of [Ymir]?*" (Faulkes)

The gods denied that Ymir was one of them but maintained that Ymir had indeed produced the first people. Snorri Sturluson, writing as a Christian, laid his finger on the implausibility that the ancient Norse, as believers, would not have spotted.

The Nine Worlds

When Odin and his brothers killed the giant Ymir, they used his body to build the cosmos. In this universe there were nine worlds, each of which houses a separate kind of being. The worlds were more or less laid out in three levels: Asgard, the god's dwelling, was the highest and most inaccessible; Midgard, where humans live, was everyday reality; and Hel was the afterworld for anyone who didn't die gloriously.

The great tree Yggdrasil was the axis mundi, the central pole that held all the worlds together. It was either of ash or yew, and was kept watered by the Norns, who continually drew water from their well to sprinkle on its roots. At the top of the tree was a giant eagle, who made the wind by flapping its wings. A dragon lived in the roots of the tree, and the squirrel Ratatosk ran up and down carrying insults between them.

The actual name of the tree, Yggdrasil, meant "Odin's horse", because he hung for nine nights and days on it when he sacrificed himself to himself, to get the runes. The World Tree was associated with the shaman's journey in most traditions; the shaman went up or down it to enter other worlds. What species of tree it was has been a matter of controversy, since some sources called it an ash, while others described it as evergreen. (It could be an ash that never loses its leaves because of the Norns who look after it.) Another name for Yggdrasil was Mimameithr, the tree or post of Mimi, probably Mimir, whose head was buried in a well under one the tree's roots. There were, in fact, three wells, each with a root of Yggdrasil attached to it. One was the place where Mimir's head was kept, another was the well of Urth, the chief of the three Norns, and the third was Hvergelmir (Heaving Kettle?), in Hel.

Apart from Yggdrasil, there were other ways between the worlds. The rainbow bridge Bifrost led from Midgard to the homes of the gods. Heimdall guarded this bridge, from his house called Himinbiorg, at Bifrost's end. To enter Hel, one had to cross the river Gjoll and its bridge, which was covered in glowing gold. A woman called Modgud guarded the bridge there, and Hel itself had a gate at its entrance.

Asgard was the home of the sky-gods (Æsir). It was the highest of all the worlds, and when Odin and Frigg sat on their high thrones they could see all that happened in the nine worlds.

Midgard was the world where humans live. The name suggests that it was between Asgard and Hel, which would have been the sky and underworld. Hel was the domain of those who die ingloriously. It varied in descriptions between being a very depressing place and an abode of light. Certainly when Baldr went there it seemed to take on some of his beauty. Odin went to Hel to raise a dead völva and learn from her what he had to do to save his son.

Nifhelheim was the place of primal ice. All things began in the gap between it and Muspellheim. The ship of the dead would set sail from there at Ragnarok, according to the *Völuspá*. Jotunheim was the home of the giants, known as jotuns or etins. Their domain was far from Asgard, and a traveller had to cross much rocky and barren terrain to get there.

Alfheim was where the light-elves (alfs) lived. Freyr is the ruler of Alfheim, which was given him as a tooth-gift (a present to a teething baby).

Svartalfheim was said to be the place where the dark-elves lived. One line of the *Skaldskaparmal* does say that there was a world of dark-elves, which presumably was this one. It doesn't say anything about it, except that Loki went there to get gold from a dwarf.

Muspellheim was the place of primal fire. This, along with Nifhelheim, was the original matrix out of which everything was born. In the myths, when Ragnarok came, Surt with his fiery blade would lead all the fire-demons to battle.

Vanaheim was the island home of the Vanir. Freya, Freyr and Njord lived there. After the war of the deities, the Æsir sent Hoenir and Mimir there, but the Vanir killed Mimir and sent his head back, because for all his wisdom he never said anything.

Cosmology: Sun, Moon and Stars

After Odin and his two brothers created the worlds, they got a giantess called Night, and her son, Day, to ride through the sky and divide the 24-hour day in two. Night's third husband was named Delling, whose name means "the Shining". He may be the same dwarf as one whose "door" was a kenning for dawn. That would fit with his role as Day's father.

The sun and the moon came next in the order of creation. Originally they were sparks thrown out by the fires of Muspellheim, but Odin and his brothers put two people to work driving chariots carrying these sparks. These people were the children of a giant called Mondilfare (World-turner) and he had named them after the sun and moon: Sól and Mani. The gods took them away to punish him for this presumption. Two wolves chased the luminaries, and at the end of the world they would catch them and eat them. While the sun's role would be taken over by her daughter in the new world that followed this cataclysm, the *Völuspá* does not mention any successor to the moon.

There are several myths which relate to the stars, mostly about the names of constellations. The two stars known as Thjazi's Eyes were placed in the sky by Odin, who put them there to recompense his daughter Skadhi after the Æsir killed Thjazi. The giant Aurvandil lost his toe to frostbite, and so Thor put it in the sky as a star. Orion's Belt was called Frigg's Distaff by the Swedes, and Ursa Major Frigg's Wain, although why we don't know.

Another aspect of Norse cosmology is the symbolism attached to cardinal directions. The main expression of this is the section of the *Grímnismál* which states:

*"They also took his [Ymir's] skull, and made out of it
the sky and set it up over the earth with four points,
and under each they set a dwarf. Their names are
Austri, Vestri, Nordri, Sudri."* (Faulkes)

Many fortresses such as Trelleborg in Denmark were
divided into four by the interior roads, which meet in the
centre, and seem to be divided by the cardinal directions.

To the Norse it seemed that south indicated culture and
civilisation, while the north stood for the opposite. Given
the geography of Scandinavia, this shouldn't surprise
anyone. North was the Arctic, south was the rest of
Europe. Notice also how in the origin myths, the north is
the location of Niflheim, which is cold and dark, while in
the south Muspellheim is bright and hot. East was the
direction of settlement, while the west was where Iceland
and Greenland were. The giants supposedly lived in the
east, as the *Prose Edda, Lokasenna, Völuspá* and
Hárbarthsljód show. The west, however, seems to have
very few associations, and no consistent place in myth.

War of the Gods

There seems to be some confusion about the origins of
the Æsir. Snorri Sturluson says that they came from
Troy, clearly trying to hitch the sky-gods to the story of
Brutus, who left the destroyed city to found Rome. From
Troy they came to the North, and since they were from
Asia, they were called Æsir. This story is part of his effort
to make the gods into humans who, as he put it:

*"whatever countries they passed through, great glory
was spoken of them, so that they seemed more like
gods than men."* (Faulkes)

After a war with the Vanir, whose origins he doesn't specify, they lived together peacefully. In the *Yngling Saga* the Æsir go to war with the Vanir, but first one side and then the other prevailed. When they decided that their lands were being destroyed, they made peace and exchanged hostages to ensure good faith. Njord and Freyr of the Vanir were traded for Mimir and Hoenir. The Vanir were not best pleased by this, because while Mimir always gave Hoenir advice, Hoenir would not tell anyone what it was. So the Vanir sent Mimir's head to the Æsir, but Odin worked magic on it, and he took counsel with it every day from then on.

The *Völuspá*, which is part of the older *Poetic Edda*, tells a different and more detailed story. In this version, the Æsir were on the scene from the beginning, organising the cosmos and building their halls. This seemed to be a time of peace, when they:

> [p]layed at draughts in the garth: right glad they
> were, nor aught lacked they of lustrous gold-
> (Hollander)

This is similar to Snorri's *Edda*, which says that the Æsir had all their furniture and tools of gold, and so it was called the golden age. After this three maidens came from Giantland, who in some way seemed to begin the destruction of paradise. (Most writers think they are the Norns, who introduce fate and time into the golden age, and thus end it.)

Nor was the Æsir's fate long in arriving. The Vanir sent Gullveig (Gold-Drunk) to them, and they tried to kill her by burning and with spears, but failed. Some authors see Gullveig as Freya, coming among the Æsir to sow discord in that guise. As the goddess of wealth, the name "Gold-Drunk" would suit her powers, and her ability to cause wars was exploited later by Odin in the *Sörla thattr*. Gullveig survived her ordeal, and was apparently reborn, taking on the new identity of the sorceress Heith.

The Æsir then held a conference to decide whether they should "*a truce/with tribute buy*" (Hollander) or else allow the Vanir their share of the sacrifices given by humans. This is Lee Hollander's version of the conflict anyway, and it fits with other Indo-European myths where the representatives of fertility and production have to fight or otherwise win their way into receiving the sacrifices given to the more aristocratic gods. Despite these constructive ideas for solving the conflict, apparently there was an actual war between the Æsir and Vanir.

The *Völuspá* tells us that:

> *His spear had Othin*   *sped o'er the host;*
> *the first of feuds was*   *thus fought in the world;*
> *was broken in battle*   *the breastwork of Asgarth,*
> *fighting Vanir*   *trod the field of battle.*

The spear-throwing was a typical part of a battle; it consecrated the Vanir to Odin after they were killed in the battle. The walls of Asgard were breached by the fighting and by the powerful magic of the Vanir. This leads into another myth about how the Æsir tricked a giant into rebuilding their wall for them.

Despite this violence, the two sides finally reached a settlement, as described in Sturluson's *Skaldskaparmal*:

> *They appointed a peace-conference and made a truce by this procedure, that both sides went up to a vat and spat their spittle into it. But when they dispersed the gods kept this symbol of truce and decided not to let it be wasted, and out of it they made a man. His*

name was Kvasir, and he was so wise that no one could ask him any question to which he did not know the answer. (Faulkes)

Kvasir died in this same myth, although he appeared in another myth, which takes place later in the scheme, and found Loki when he went into hiding.

Some authors see this as a myth of an actual battle or social conflict. They see the Vanir as the representatives of an earlier, pastoral society who worshipped gods of fertility alone. The Æsir are identified with a warlike, patriarchal Indo-European group who invade and disrupt this peaceful lifestyle. (Although, as Turville-Petre points out, the *Völuspá* seems to show that the Vanir were the late-comers.[19]) I think that the myth is less literal than that. This conflict at the beginning mirrors the cosmic conflict at the end of the myth, which will kill all the senior gods, but bring about a new world.

The gender politics of the myth are also less obvious than this reading allows. The goddesses are given very little place, the main actors being Odin and the hostages Njord and Hoenir. If Gullveig is Freya, then she plays a subversive part by inciting the Æsir and then becoming the seithkona Heith, who "*cast spells where she could*" (Hollander). Her power seems to have been limited to the traditional women's sphere, however, and we never hear of her again.

The Vanir in the matriarchal-feminist reading are the good deities, who are on women's side. While no one would doubt that Freya was a feminist icon, a brave and independent woman, there are more troubling aspects to the Vanir. Freyr's "courtship" of Gerd was hardly a model for male emulation; her wishes in the matter counted for nothing. She was coerced into marriage with the god, and this hardly augurs for a happy future together. On the plus side Njord said that "*he [Freyr] grieves no maiden and no man's wife*", and there were no other stories of him dallying with women. Njord also defended Freya from the criticisms of Loki, when he jeered at her for having many lovers, saying "*Who cares how a few husbands came to be cuckolds?*" (Terry) Presumably he felt that Loki had no business criticising her conduct.

The other problem with the Vanir is that there aren't many goddesses among them. The only one we know of is Freya. Njord's wife/sister is not named, and she is only mentioned once. Often authors try to make up for this by either marrying Njord to the goddess mentioned by Tacitus, Nerthus, or making Frigg a Vanir. If Nerthus was still worshipped at the time when the Eddas were written, there is no mention of it. As for Frigg, she was very definitely an Æsir. The only criterion for including her is that she is a female, and therefore should be associated with fertility. It certainly isn't supported by the sources.

It's probably not fair to say that the Æsir had more goddesses, since there were more of them altogether. However, there were many goddesses among them, and they mostly fill roles typical of Indo-European abstractions. (So do many of the gods, like Forseti.) The gods sometimes expressed attitudes towards women that we would find hard to accept, such as Odin's boast that he tricked seven maidens into his bed. Still, their attitudes were not so different from those of the Vanir. Freyr was a warrior god as well, after all, and the way he won Gerd is not exactly a model of mutuality. Odin's marriage with Frigg, and Thor's with Sif, were certainly loving relationships. Like Njord defending Freya, Thor stood by his wife after Loki cut off her hair, which was how adulteresses were punished, and made him give her hair of gold. It is not so easy to assign blame in the myths, although certainly the desire for clear-cut good guys is understandable.

The End of the World

Just as the goddesses played a very small role in the creation of the worlds, they did not figure largely in the end of it all. The *Völuspá* sketches in the end of the worlds in brief, impressionistic scenes. The rooster Gold-comb woke the heroes in Odin's hall, who came forth to fight. Heimdall's horn sounded the alarm, and Mimir's head told Odin that the time has come. The rainbow bridge between Asgard and earth crumbled to dust, the cosmic tree Yggdrasil shook. One by one the gods went forth to fight the various menaces that spring up, and they died. (Odin's death was called Frigg's "second sorrow".) Then the wolves that ate the sun and moon ran free, and darkness covered the worlds.*"However, finally the chaos ended, and*

> *She [the seeress] sees the earth   rising again*
> *out of the waters,   green once more;*
> *an eagle flies   over rushing waterfalls,*
> *hunting for fish   from the craggy heights."*
> (Terry)

Then the new gods appeared, and read the runes to learn what the new world held for them. The new gods is an accurate phrase, because almost all of them were the sons of the Æsir, Baldr, Magni and Modhi and some others. The only goddess that survived the cataclysm was the sun's daughter, who now rode the sky in her mother's stead.

There is some suspicion among scholars that this whole episode is part of a post-Christian harmonising of the

Biblical revelation and Norse myth. The idea of a periodic destruction followed by renewal is not exclusive to the Christians, however. The same idea appears in Hindu belief. With its return to a paradisiacal golden age, the Norse myth ties together two of humanity's greatest beliefs, that life was once perfect, and can become perfect again.

Goddesses

High said: "There are no less than twelve Æsir whose nature is divine."
Then spoke Just-as-high: "No less holy are the Asyniur, nor is their power any less." (Faulkes)

The goddesses of the Germanic people are not so well-known as the gods, nor do we have as much information about them. By the Viking period, society had become very warlike and male-dominated, so that although some goddesses were prominent, most were merely names. All the same, there are some things we know about them that are worth mentioning.

First, there are no triple goddesses of the Wiccan type among the Germanic goddesses. The Norns are definitely three in number, but there is no evidence that they were maiden, mother and crone. In general, there do not seem to be any goddesses of old age. A person followed the same deity all her lifetime, and this deity did not change with age. One's patron goddess seems to have been determined by sexual status. Frigg looked after wives, Freya after unmarried women, and Gefjon after virgins.

Second, there is no moon-goddess. The moon is a god, and the sun is his sister. This may seem obvious to anyone who already knows some of these myths, but it is amazing how many books either wish this fact out of existence or announce that some other goddess is "really" the moon. This is disrespectful to the people that created these myths and believed them, and tells us more about the author's rigidity of thought than about the Germans.

Thirdly, Frigg and Freya are not the same goddess. Some authors seem to think that they go together as the wife/mistress of Odin, but their differences are obvious. Frigg upholds the wife in her household, and deals with the domestic side of life. Freya is promiscuous and rules both love and battle. Frigg is a peace- making goddess, since wives were often the family peacemakers. Freya, on the other hand, often appears in the sources as a bringer of conflict. One is a sky-goddess, one is a fertility deity. People who confuse them do so because they can't see past the mutual connection to Odin, defining them both by their sexual relations.

Finally, the numerous goddesses whose function is summed up in their names, like Syn and Vor, are often dismissed as mere abstractions. They are nothing of the kind. If these authors knew anything about Indo-European mythology, they would know that it is full of abstract deities who fulfil various functions. The Romans, Indians and Iranians also had lots of deities who did one specific thing, which their names reflected. These varied from fairly important ones, like Mitra ("contract") and Janus, who took on other functions over time, to minor ones like the Zoroastrian Spenta Mainyu ("Beneficent Spirit").

Frigg

(Old Norse Frigg, Old High German Frija, Lombard Frea, Anglo- Saxon Frig)

Frigg is the queen of the goddesses, and Odin's wife. This makes sense, since her name means "the beloved", and

Odin is "*the dweller in Frigg's bosom*". Although some mistakenly identify her as the earth to Odin's sky, she is as much a heavenly deity as her husband. She is one of the sky-deities, the Æsir, and there is nothing about her which suggests that she has power over fertility. Her father was Fjorgyn, a rather mysterious god. There is no mention of her mother in the *Eddas*. She sits with Odin on the high throne from which they can see all that passes in all the worlds.

She lives in her own hall, Fensalir ("Sea-hall") with her attendants Eir, Saga, Gna, and Fulla. In her hall she sits and spins, which relates to women's economic activities. (Women in the pre- Modern ages often ran their own businesses and kept the profits.) The spinning is also part of her function as a sky-goddess, since she spins the clouds. According to the Swedes her spindle is also a constellation, Frigg's Distaff, around which the stars turn and the universe is woven. Like Freya she has a cloak of feathers, taken from hawks and falcons, although we never hear of her flying about in it.

There is abundant proof that Frigg was an ancient goddess, whose worship was as old as that of Thor or Odin, yet few places can be found that held her temples. Some have been found in Sweden, such as *Frigg-jarakr (Frigg's Cornfield) in Västergotland.[20] Branston has claimed to find some others in England, such as Freefolk, Froyle, Frobury, and Fryup.[21] A charter from tenth-century England mentions lists Friden in Derbyshire as Frigedene, "valley of Frig".[22] Her importance is attested by the number of attendant goddesses or alternate selves who surround her. The Germans must have thought highly of her, since they named Friday after her.[23] (All of the days of the week are named after deities.)

Frigg and births

In *The Plaint of Oddrun*, Borgny says, after she has given birth:

> May hallowed wights   bring help to thee,
> Frigg and Freya,   and favoring gods
> as off thou warded   evil from me...
> (Hollander)

Since Frigg was the goddess of married women, it is not surprising that she was invoked to bless women during births. (In this instance, however, Borgny is thanking the midwife, not asking for assistance.) While the two goddesses are here invoked to aid in childbirth, Hollander says that the mention of Freya is a mistake, since it was Frigg who was normally called on in these matters.[24] However, since both are goddesses of women, both would be logical choices for any situation where women needed help.

Foresight

In the *Lokasenna*, when Loki slanders Frigg, Freya defends her:

> Thou art raving, Loki,   to reckon up
> all the ill thou hast done:
> I ween that Frigg   the fates knoweth,
> though she say it not herself.
> (Hollander)

The Prologue to the *Snorri's Edda* also tells us that Frigg had the gift of prophecy. This is in addition to the knowledge she gains by her seat on the high throne; this is the prophecy that the Germans believed was the province of women. In the *Vafthrúdismál* Odin asks her advice about a trip to the land of the giants, so it seems her ability to prophecy and advise was respected by the other Æsir.

This fore-knowledge has tragic consequences when she foresees the death of her son Baldr. All the same, she tries to save him by action; she gets all living things to promise not to hurt him. However, once again Loki is in her way. He disguises himself as an old woman, and learns from Frigg that she didn't bother with the mistletoe because it seemed harmless. Immediately he makes a mistletoe stake and gives it to blind Hod to throw at Baldr. (Baldr's invulnerability had given the Æsir a new sport; watching weapons bounce off him.) The mistletoe kills Baldr, and he has to descend to Hel until after Ragnarok. This death is the first of Frigg's sorrows, the second being Odin's death when the doom of the gods comes.

Wife and mother

Frigg's power is that of the bonds which marriage and family bring about. In our time a housewife is not someone of exalted position, but once they were the peacemakers of the family, as well as the economic managers. The more prosperous had to supervise the activities of the servants, as well as making their own contributions to the family's well-being. As a token of her status, Frigg carries a bunch of keys on her belt. (Women wore these as a symbol of authority, even if a housekeeper actually controlled the stores.) In Sweden, Thursday was her day, and the house was prepared for the visit of Frigg and Thor: "*Hallow the god Thor and Frigg*". On that day no one could spin or use a distaff, since Frigg was spinning. Sometimes people saw an old man and a woman sitting at her distaff; Thor in his elder aspect, and the goddess.

Frigg had much in common with other Indo-European goddesses who were wives and mothers. The Greek Hera and the Roman Juno were very similarly placed, since both were in the First Lady position. All three were invoked to make wives fertile, and were worshipped by matrons. Juno, like Frigg, was also a somewhat independent goddess who had her own powers and cult. Hera was less powerful than either of those two. While Frigg had the gift of prophecy herself, Hera could grant it to those she favoured, as she did with the horse Xanthus. Both goddesses advised their husbands on their affairs. The interesting difference between Hera and Frigg is that unlike the Greek goddess, Frigg takes Odin's infidelities calmly. Perhaps the Asyunia feels more secure in her position than the jealous Olympian, or it may reflect the more equal marriages of Northerners.

Another side to Frigg

Despite her image as the good housewife, there are some rather odd myths about Frigg. Saxo Grammaticus says that she had part of a gold statue melted down so she could have a gold necklace. Unfortunately the statue was of Odin, and he had enchanted it to tell if anyone vandalised it. So she slept with one of her servants in exchange for having the statue melted down so it couldn't accuse her. Odin was so disgusted when he found out that he left her. He left mith-Othin to rule in his stead, and only came back when she had died.

This episode may be what Loki was referring to when he said:

Hush thee, Frigg,   *who art Fjorgyn's daughter:*
thou hast ever been mad after men.
Vili and Vé   *thou, Vithrir's [Odin's] spouse,*
didst fold to thy bosom both.
(Hollander)

Vili and Vé were Odin's two brothers or other aspects, so it hardly seems fair of Loki to accuse Frigg of adultery with Odin's other selves. Perhaps Mith-othin was the same as the two other "Odins" and so Frigg is blameless in both cases.

Frigg vs. Odin

Unlike the Greek goddess Hera, Frigg is rarely shown arguing with Odin or plotting against him. However, occasionally she did oppose him. Again, unlike Hera, she tended to be successful when she put her will against her husband's. The history of the Lombards is one such myth, where she arranges matters so that Odin comes to favour them over the Vandals. She told the Winniles to come to Odin at sunrise, with the women wearing their long hair over their faces. She then turned Odin's bed so it faced east. When he woke in the morning he no longer faced the Vandals, his favourites, but the Winniles. He looked at them and asked who these Longbeards were. Frigg then told him that having named them, he had to give them victory.

Odin and Frigg also contend over their favourites in the introduction to *Grímnismál*. He goes to visit his favourite Gerriod, in disguise. Frigg tells him that a deceiver is coming, and so Gerriod puts Odin on a roasting-spit by the fire for nine nights. As a result Odin comes to give the kingship to her favourite, Agnar.

Frígg, Hlín and other goddesses

In the Völuspá, the seeress refers to Frigg by a by-name, Hlín:

Another woe   *awaiteth Hlín,*
When forth goes Othin   *to fight the Wolf,*
and the slayer of Beli   *to battle with Surt:*
then Frigg's husband   *will fall lifeless.*
(Hollander)

However, there is another reference to Hlín, this time in Snorri Sturluson's list of the Asyniur. He seems to think that she is an independent goddess, although part of Frigg's retinue. She is supposed to save people from peril if Frigg favours them. While the name Hlín is often used in kennings for women, Frigg rarely is mentioned. If Frigg and Hlín were the same goddess, this would make Frigg and Freya equal in the number of times skalds mention them.[25]

As for the other goddesses that make up Frigg's retinue (Eir, Saga, Fulla, Lofn, Gna), they are often said to be hypostates of Frigg. (A hypostatis of a goddess is another form of her, emanating from the original form, but only having part of its power.) If this is so, Frigg must have been a more important goddess than the poetic sources indicate. (Insignificant deities do not get multiplied by their followers.) All of them perform tasks for Frigg, rather than having a separate function. Despite this, they all should be seen as goddesses in their own rights, since even a hypostasis of a goddess is also a goddess. Snorri is in no doubt that they are goddesses, rather than just aspects of Frigg, and perhaps he knew what he was talking about.

41

Frigg and Friday

One of the confusions of Norse and German mythology is the uncertainty over which goddess, Frigg or Freya, had Friday named after her. That Friday was named after one of them is certain, since all the other days are named after deities (Sól, Mani, Tyr/Tiw, Odin/Woden, Thor, Saeter). The Germanic peoples probably got the idea of naming days after deities from the Romans, who named theirs after Sól, Luna, Mars, Mercury, Jupiter, Venus and Saturn. The German deities were clearly matched to the Roman ones in terms of functions.

Venus, then, was matched with either Frigg or Freya. Freya was the Norse and German goddess of love, but the linguistic evidence shows that it was Frigg who was allocated Friday. In the OE frigadaez, OHG Friadag, Old Frisian Frigendei and OI Frjgádagr, the root *frijo- meaning "beloved, loving" appears, which is also the root of Frigg's name. In an English sermon, Ælfric preached against false gods:

> And the sixth day is dedicate to that shameless goddess called Venus, and Frigc in Danish.[26]

Apparently the Norse and Germans valued the love of marriage over passionate love, and it is true that the sagas and myths have little to say on this subject.

Freya
(ON Freyja, OHG Frowe, German Frau)

According to Snorri's *Edda*, Freya was "the most glorious of the Asyniur". In the *Ynglinga Saga* it says: *"Freya held to the sacrifices for she alone of the gods still lived. She then became so very renowned, that they called all noble* women by her name, even as they are now called fruer; so every woman is called Freya (Frue) who rules over her own property, but she is called house-freya (husfrue) who has a household." [27] Clearly then she was a goddess of some importance, who symbolised femininity for the Norse. Her name means "Lady", which like Freyr (Lord) is an honourary title. She has other names, such as Mardoll (Sea-Brightness), Horn (Flax), Syr (Sow), and Gefn (Generous One). She rides about in a chariot pulled by two cats called Bygul (Bee-gold) and Trjegul (tree-gold/amber).

Her home in Asgard was on the plain called Folkvangr (Battlefield), in a hall called Sessrumnir (Many-Seated). She rode to battle each day as the leader of the Valkyries, sharing the souls of the slain with Odin. Interestingly, Freya got not only half the dead, but first pick of the fallen heroes. This may have been her reward for teaching Odin seithr, a form of magic many link to shamanism. (She uses her magic in *Hyndludjoth* so that Ottar will win his court case, even reversing Hyndla's curse on him.) She also received the souls of unmarried women, since she was their patron. Some women in the sagas kill themselves when their lovers die so that they can go to Freya's hall. In the *Ynglinga Saga* she is a priestess of the gods, who maintained the rites.

Comparisons

Freya has similarities with goddesses of other cultures. Like the Irish Maeve, Morrigan and Macha, she is warlike and sexual, willing to use magic or trickery to get her way. All four goddesses haunted battlefields, Freya as a Valkyrie and the Irish deities in their war-goddess capacity. The Morrigan, Macha and Badb could become ravens or crows, while Freya had a falcon shape. Maeve, like Freya, was intensely promiscuous, saying that she had never had a lover without another in his shadow. Like the Valkyries, the Morrigan promised victory to Cú Chulainn if he slept with her. All four were potent in magic.

Like Aphrodite, she is a goddess of sex and love, rather than motherhood. Similarly, although both are married, their spouses are unimportant to their legends. Aphrodite's kestos, which gave its wearer the power of sexual attractiveness, can be compared to Freya's necklace. Freya slept with four dwarves to get it, and Lotte Motz compares this with Aphrodite's marriage to Hephestios, another ugly smith. The story of Adonis, and how Aphrodite lost him for part of each year, is similar to that of Freya and her wandering husband Od. Both goddesses were promiscuous, with no blame attaching to them for this. Freya is warlike, but the closest the Greek goddess comes to this is with her favourite lover, Ares. The two of them are also associated with gold and jewels: Freya wears a precious necklace, and her daughters are both called "Treasure", while the Homeric Hymns to Aphrodite describe her jewellery several times.

Another goddess she is frequently compared to is Cybele, worshipped by the Phrygians. Both goddesses were linked to rites involving unmanly men. Cybele's priests were the galli, who cut their testicles off during an annual festival and afterward dressed as women. The seithr-men were frequently called unmanly by the macho Norsemen, much the same reaction as the galli aroused in the Romans. Cybele rode a chariot pulled by lions, while Freya's was drawn by cats. Both were involved in war: Freya was the head Valkyrie, and in Virgil's *Aenid* the hero prayed to Cybele to "be now a leader for me in battle"[28].

The Hittites, an Indo-European people who lived in what is now Turkey, had many goddesses with Freya-like attributes. The head goddess, Hebat, had a lion as her attribute, as did Kubaba, who later became Cybele. The goddess Sauska wore wings and carried arms, showing that she was a war-goddess.

Outside the Indo-European community, the goddesses Anat, Ishtar and Inanna are also likened to Freya, who embodied both sexual and warlike energies. Both the Ugaritic Anat and Freya had their brothers for lovers (Baal also means "Lord"), and were warlike goddesses. Anat also flew like a bird. Like the gory Valkyries, Anat waded in blood in one myth. Ishtar and Innana were both extremely erotic goddesses, whose hymns described their sexual encounters in detail. Like Freya they grieved for their lovers when they died. The Code of Hammurabi calls Innana "Mistress of the Battlefield"[29], which fits with Freya the Valkyrie. All of them, like Freya with Ottar, protected kings.

Freya and Odin

Freya and Odin were deities with many things in common, which may be why the myths said they are married, despite Odin's marriage to Frigg. Both were deceitful: Odin was known for betraying people who placed their trust in him, while according to the *Yngling Saga* Freya *"was of shifty mind"*[30]. Both of them used sex to get what they want, and saw no reason why they shouldn't. Odin slept with Gerriod to get the mead of inspiration, and enchanted Rind into sleeping with him so that Vali could be born and avenge Baldr's death. Freya slept with four dwarves so that she could have the magical necklace Brisingamen. Neither of them was particularly faithful, since Odin had many liaisons with mortals, goddesses and giantesses, while Freya had apparently slept with all the gods, including her brother.

Both of them travelled through the worlds, although the myths never actually showed Freya using her falcon form. (Odin supposedly could turn into various animals and send that form to far places.) Loki borrowed Freya's cloak to rescue Idunn from a giant. Odin used many names in his travels, and one explanation for the many synonyms for Freya was that she also wandered, when she sought for her husband Odr. This Odr may be the same as Odin, although in the myth he vanished each winter, which caused Freya to weep tears of amber and gold as she went south to search for him. This seems out of character for Odin, and I propose another explanation below.

Goddess of love

Freya was also the goddess of love, and prayed to by all who were in love. She enjoyed the reciting of love-poetry, and her name is the basis of the verb "to court". As proof of her desirability several giants tried to carry her off, although none succeeded. Also, Loki accuses her of having slept with all the elves and all the gods, including her brother Freyr. Of course, Njord her father points out that sibling marriage was allowed among the Vanir, while the Æsir found it repulsive. Another who taunted her was the giantess Hyndla, who taunted her:

> *in the night who runnest-*   *thou noble friend-*
> *in her heat as Heithrún*   *the he-goats among.*
> (Hollander)

(Heithrún was a nanny-goat mentioned in *Grímnismál*.)

Despite Loki's accusations, she had her limits, as the gods found out when a giant demanded her as ransom for Thor's hammer.

> Wroth grew Freya, foamed with rage;
> the shining halls shook with her wrath,
> the Brisings' necklace burst asunder:
> "Most mad after men thou mayst call me,
> If I wend with thee to the world of the etins."
> (Hollander)

The difference seems to be that Freya chooses her own lovers, and is angered by the Æsir's attempts to use her as a pawn in their games.

Goddess of fertility?

It is well-established in the Eddas that Freyr is a god who gives good harvests and protects farmers. However, nowhere does it say that Freya has a similar function. Out of the Vanir deities, Njord "rules the winds" and so people prayed to him for successful sea-voyages or when fishing, Freyr ruled "the prosperity of the earth", and Freya apparently is a love-goddess. The connection between the three is not that they are fertility-oriented, but wealth-giving. Snorri states that all three can make their worshippers prosperous.

In the chapter on the petroglyphs I discussed some reasons why the Norse seem to have viewed fertility as a male rather than female attribute. The misattribution of fertility to Freya is probably a result of an underlying belief that female deities, especially sexually active ones, have to be fecund. Even the Greek Aphrodite is often called a fertility goddess, when it is obviously Demeter who makes the crops grow. (If it was Aphrodite who gave fertility, then the myth of Demeter and Persephone would have no point.)

Goddess of wealth

Freya as a wealth-giving deity has many connections to money, jewels and general prosperity. She has two daughters, both named "Treasure", she weeps gold and amber, which are both precious substances, and as one of the Vanir she gives prosperity to humans. Her necklace, Brisingamen, was made of either gold or amber, and was her most famous possessions. To get it, she had to sleep with each of the four dwarves who made it. Later Loki stole it from her to give to Odin. To get it back Freya had to agree to instigate a battle between two kings so that Valhalla could be filled with the dead. Another story seems to be that Loki stole it but Heimdall either prevented him or fought him and won it back. There are hints of this in the *Eddas* but the actual story has been lost.

Valkyrie Goddess

Freya is also famous for her warlike nature. She received half of all slain heroes, as well as getting first choice (while Odin got the other half to fill his hall, Valhalla). Every day she rode to battle, according to *Grímnismál*, to make her choices, and one of her names was Val-Freya.[31] (Val- from valr, "the host of the slain".) In the *Sorla thattr* she is employed by Odin to stir up eternal war, and she does so in the guise of Göndul, which is also the name of a Valkyrie and appears in kennings for battle. One translation of Folkvangr, Freya's home, is "Battlefield", and her boar is called Hildisvíni, the boar of battle. Else Mundal suggests that the Valkyries should be attached to

Freya rather than Odin, in line with her theory that the lower and higher goddesses form a continuum. (See the chapter "Nornir, Fygliur and Valkyriur" for more on this.)

Her bravery is attested in the following passage:

> ...he said he was going to remove Val-hall and take it to Giantland, but bury Asgard and kill all the gods, except that he was going to take Freyia and Sif home with him, and Freyia was the only one then who dared to bring him drink...(Faulkes)

This makes Freya the most courageous among all the gods and goddesses except Thor, who smites the presumptuous giant. Another passage mentioned above tells how the gods had to abandon a plan to marry Freya to a giant after her wrath shook Asgard. Clearly she was not a goddess to trifle with.

The *Sörla thattr* shows her causing a war, and perhaps taking on a Valkyrie form. This came about because Loki stole her necklace, and Odin made her start the war before he gives it back. (This tale also tells how she had to sleep with four dwarves to get it in the first place.) Then either a Valkyrie named Göndul (named in the *Völuspá* and several kennings for battle) or Freya in disguise appeared to King Hethin, and induced him to visit Högni.

While Hethin was there, the woman appeared to him, gave him a horn of ale to enchant him, and induced him to kill Högni's wife and steal his only daughter. He saw Göndul again after that, but in the other form of the Valkyrie, as a large, dark shadow. The men fought, dying and being resurrected by magic, for 143 years.

Freya as sun-goddess

Freya is also a solar goddess, who seems to have absorbed some of Sól's power. That she weeps gold and amber (the names of her cats), which are solar materials, and wears a necklace of some glittering material is proof of this. In Sweden a folk-song called her *den väna solen* - "the beautiful sun".[32] The myth of her search for Odr also fits with her solar nature. She goes south to warmer lands to rescue him and then returns in spring, bringing new life. If this was a god it would immediately be proof of his solar identity.

Worship of Freya

She was a popular goddess, worshipped especially in Sweden and Norway. People called on her for help, for instance in *Hálfs saga* King Alfrek set up a contest between his two wives to see who could brew the best beer. One called on Freya, and the other on Odin. (The one Odin supported won, of course.) One author counts between 20 and 30 place-names that indicate her worship in Norway alone. Three can be traced back to *Frejuhof (Freya's temple) and others are compounds with words for meadow, land, etc..[33] In Sweden her name appears in *Freyjuvé (Freya's sanctuary/temple) and Freyjulundr (Freya's grove), as well as perhaps Frøal and Fröale, which might be associated with Gothic alhs, Old. Engl. ealhi, meaning "temple". Sweden also knew her under her by-name Horn, in Hornarvé.[34]

Gefjon

This goddess has a rather paradoxical nature. Sturluson described her a "maiden" and says that all maidens go to her when they die. Various writers compare her to Athena or Vesta, which also implies that she was a virgin.

How does this reconcile with the following accusation, which Loki hurls at her:

> I know a youth   who gave you a necklace-
>   you laid a leg over him! (Terry)

The origin story of Zeeland, also, says that Gefjon got the land from King Gylfi in return for "entertaining" him. So is she a virgin or isn't she?

Apparently the Norse, at least those who wrote, saw her as a virgin. This seems to be the meaning of the passage in the *Volsa thattr* in which a maiden says:

> I swear by Gefjon
> and the other gods
> that I enforced take the red phallus.[35]

Gefjon is interpreted by Christian writers as chaste, since they are the ones who gloss her as Graeco-Roman maiden goddesses.

On the other side of the argument, Gefjon means "the giving one", and this is often understood to be a sexual reference. The myth (in *Gylfaginning* and *Yngling Saga*) of her visit to King Gylfi also assumes that she slept with him. (It seems that in all dealings with the gods, Gylfi was doomed to be the loser.) Either at Odin's instigation or on her own, she visits the king in the guise of a tramp, and after "entertaining" him, he grants her all the land she can plow. So she either then takes four oxen and ploughs a cut so deep that the land breaks off from Norway and becomes Seeland. Or, in the *Yngling Saga*, she goes off, has a giant father four large sons for her, and disguises them as the oxen. In gratitude, Odin marries her to his son Skjoldr.

Another point cited in favour of her non-maiden status is her similarity to, if not identity with, Freya. Since one of Freya's by-names was Gefn, "Giver", it is not surprising that people confuse them. Also, both of them take the dead, although Freya takes warriors and women who kill themselves, while Gefjon takes unmarried women. The necklace story, as Loki tells it, links them, since Freya had sex with four dwarves in exchange for the magic Brisingamen. The sacrifice offered to Gefjon in the *Bretasögur* is similar to the one given Freya in the *Hyndlujoth*. However, I don't see this evidence as overwhelming. If Freya and Gefjon are one goddess, why are they always mentioned separately? Even if they were originally one, they seem to be quite distinct in the sources. (Frigg is also accused of having traded sex for a necklace. This myth seems to be unsure which goddess it belongs to.)

As for Gefjon's chastity, there is no reason to suppose that she can't be a maiden. There is no proof that she had sex with Gylfi. The story that she slept with a giant and married Odin's son comes in a late source, with dubious connections to other myths. Of course, there are many other explanations. Gefjon may have exercised the deity's privilege of embodying a value and its opposite. She may have had renewable virginity. Lotte Motz says that the word for maiden, maer, could indicate either a virgin or an unmarried woman,[36] so perhaps it's a moot point.

Miriam Dexter-Robbins put forward the idea that Gefjon was a virgin in terms of her function.[37] Figures of sovereignty were usually virgin, which symbolised the intact nature of the land, like the Irish goddess Flaith. She would fit into a long line of goddesses of sovereignty, since she handed over a kingdom to Odin (although instead of marrying him, she married his son). By marrying his son, however, she founded a dynasty of kings, the Scyldings. So she produced rulers, after giving them something to rule.

Apart from its evidence about Gefjon's virginity, the Gylfi story is significant because it reverses the usual pattern in Norse myth, where the gods go into giantland and get giantesses pregnant, while the goddesses are to be kept from the giants. She breaks the taboo against the women crossing social boundaries, and so sets herself apart from the other goddesses. Firstly because, unlike Freya, she does not view the giants with loathing. Second, she goes to them of her own will, unlike Idunn. Finally, she uses them to serve her ends, just as Odin might do. Her independence is unusual.

She must have been a more important goddess that the sources indicate, who received worship and sacrifice. She appeared in a later saga, the *Bretasögur*, in which Brutus, the great-grandson of Aneas, found on an island a temple of Saturnus, Jupiter and Gefjon. He sacrificed a cow to the goddess, walked round her image and asked her about his future. He then went to sleep in the temple, and Gefjon told him in a dream that he would have a powerful kingdom.[38] Outside of saga evidence, place-names show that she was worshipped by the Danes at places like Gevnø and Gentofte.[39]

A final point of interest about Gefjon is the identity of her lover in the *Lokasenna*. Her husband is Skjold, or Scyld, who may be the same as the boy-king who floated to Denmark with a sheaf of wheat in his hand (from which his name comes). It would be odd, though, if Loki taunted her about him. Hollander suggests that it may be Heimdall, who was often called the white god. Some translations of the poem do say that Gefjon slept with a white or bright youth. The commonest idea is that it was the giant she got her four sons from, although it would be odd to describe a giant as bright. Unless Hollander is right, it must be some other liaison, which is lost to us.

Skaдhí

Thazji, Skadhi's father, was the giant who stole Idunn. When he was killed the giantess came down from her mountains and demanded wergild (reparation) from the Æsir. They offered her a choice of gods to marry, and she had to select one by looking at their feet. She chose the most beautiful feet, thinking they were Baldr's, but they were Njord's. Next the Æsir had to get her to laugh, which she doubted they could do. However, Loki tied his testicles to a nanny-goat's beard, and the tug of war made them both squeal. Loki finally dropped into Skadhi's lap, and this made her laugh. To round off the atonement, Odin put her father's eyes in the sky as stars.

So Skadhi and Njord were married, but she hated his home in watery Vanaheim. Njord hated Thrymheim, which she inherited from her father, because of the snow and mountains. They divorced amicably, and she later married Ullr, god of winter. Skadhi was the goddess of skis, and a hunter.

Skadhi and Loki had it out again in the *Lokasenna*, when he taunted her about her father's death. She responded by describing to him his later fate: to be bound under the earth with his son's guts. She also told him that from her groves and shrines he will get cold comfort. When Loki was finally bound, Skadhi set a poisonous serpent to drip venom on his face.

The various myths that cluster around Skadhi suggest that she was a much more important figure that the Eddas indicated. In the *Lokasenna* she told Loki:

> *from my holy groves and hallowed shrines will cold counsel ever come for thee"*. (Hollander)

Place-names such as Skadavé (Skadhi's temple) and Skadalundr (Skadhi's grove) also indicate a strong cult of Skadhi once existed, especially in eastern Sweden.[40] The Jarls of Hladir, in northern Norway, traced their descent from a union between her and Odin, which looks like a way of connecting themselves to two of the most popular deities of their people. The son of the two deities, Saeming, was their ancestor.

Gender trouble

The story of how she married Njord had several motifs which also turned up in later folklore, and made the story a great deal more comprehensible. An Indian folktale told how a father and son had to choose their brides by their footprints, so that the son got the mother and the father the daughter.[41] Another type of folktale involved a woman who requires her suitors to make her laugh before she would marry them. Some of these involved sticking people or things together in obscene or embarrassing ways, so that the heroine would laugh at them.[42] The point is that Loki takes the place of the suitor who made her laugh, but he himself was of ambivalent gender (he bore a foal in the shape of a mare) and this may be why Skadhi laughed at him. Skadhi herself took on a male role when she stormed Asgard to avenge her father, and so both the characters in this myth were crossing gender lines.

When the Æsir offered to marry Skadhi to one of the gods, it might have been an attempt to re-feminise her. She arrived in her battle-gear, taking the male role, and the peace-process involved Loki making himself feminine. However, it was women who were traded in marriage to put a stop to hostilities between families. So the marriage offer was an astute move on the part of the Æsir, since it put Skadhi in the female role of peace-maker, and took away her initiative. Marriage was women's business, not war.

One myth that showed Skadhi acting in a womanly, motherlike fashion is the *Skírnirsmal*. The first verse had her asking Skirnir why her "son", Freyr, was acting so strange. From this we can infer two things; first, that Skadhi could act as a woman when she wanted to, and second, that despite the disharmony between her and Njord, she had amicable relations with his family.

Her marriage to Njord, however, was both a triumph and a failure. On the one hand, she succeeded where her father failed, in getting a spouse from among the gods, who normally tried to avoid such unions. However, she didn't get Odin's heir, Baldr, but a god of lesser importance. This might explain her later affair with Odin; if she couldn't marry the heir, she would try to supplant him with her own children.[43] In the sense that she becomes a goddess herself, she won. She is listed among the Asyniur, and received worship.

Skadhi's relations with Loki were more convoluted than her liaison with Odin or marriage to Njord. When she first came to Asgard, she would have been perfectly justified in killing him, but he managed to defuse her anger, as he no doubt often had to do with the Æsir. She remembered her earlier vengefulness, and when the time came to bind Loki for killing Baldr, she fitted a poisonous serpent over his head, to drip burning venom on him. However, it seemed that she once had some sort of liaison with Loki. In the *Lokasenna*, he replied to her taunt about his ultimate fate:

> *You spoke more sweetly   to Laufey's son*
> *   when you lay beside me in bed.*
> *There's a tale   well worth the telling,*
> *   if we're all to air our faults!*
> (Terry)

It was exceptionally cruel of Loki, since he had just told or reminded her of his role in her father's death, to also bring this up. The folktale motif appears again here, since it is the suitor who usually tries to make the bride-to-be laugh.

One of the more peculiar theories about Skadhi is that she was once a god who became a goddess, perhaps because Njord had once been her "wife". Gabriel Turville-Petre suggests this, pointing out that she carried weapons and did other "masculine" things. He also points out that her name was a masculine one, although nouns related to it all decline feminine, which may be simply because the Norse simply realised that the noun was the wrong gender and acted accordingly. He then goes on to wonder why a god would become a goddess, although the fact that the formerly female Njord became a god doesn't bother him. (Presumably Njord traded up, and Skadhi down, in his view.)

Independent Goddess

Skadhi, like Gefjon, tends to confound writers who want the goddesses in neat little pigeonholes. She acted independently, and unlike Freya, who was never shown in her Valkyrie role, actually put on armour to avenge her father. In the *Lokasenna*, she was the only goddess who argued back when Loki abused her. (Freya stood up for Frigg, but not herself.) Skadhi had a lot in common with the Greek Artemis. Both hunted with a bow, and both preferred the mountains and woods to the company of the other gods. Other writers call Skadhi the descendant of the Mistress of Wild Animals, a Middle Eastern goddess only identified by the animals who accompany her.

The Ultimate Mismatch

There is an odd parallel to the Njord - Skadhi marriage in the story of Hadingus in the *Gesta Danorum*. He married a woman and settled down, but finally he became discontent, and declared that he hated the mountains, and longed for the sea, where he used to sail. His wife, Regnilda, replied that she loved the woods, and the screaming gulls and crashing waves unsettled her.

Before they married, Regnilda tended his wounds after he rescued her from a giant, and sewed a ring into his leg-wound so she would know him again. Later she was to choose her husband, and felt the bodies of her suitors for the ring. When she found Hadingus's ring, she chose him.

This story goes against the theory, favoured by those who prefer to see all myths as just-so stories about nature, that Skadhi and Njord's marriage either represented the god of fertility marrying and "thawing" the goddess of winter, or else symbolising a ritual that involved a sacred marriage between a woods-goddess and a sea-god. Either way, these rituals don't seem to have been very successful, a point not addressed by those who adhere to this theory. I think that Njord and Skadhi became the paradigm of a mismatch, and therefore Saxo

Grammaticus stole the plaints of the two deities for his own unhappy couple.

Iðunn

The wife of the skald Bragi, she held the apples of immortality in her ash-wood casket. Once Loki was captured by a giant, and only got free on condition that he would return with Idunn and her apples. So he tricked her by saying that there were apples outside the walls of Asgard that she should see, and handed her over once they were outside. Then all the deities began to age, and made Loki bring her back. To do this he borrowed Freya's falcon cloak, and after turning Idunn into a nut he flew back to Asgard. The giant Thjazi flew after him as an eagle, but the wily god lured him into a bonfire the Æsir had set on Asgard's walls.

At Ragnarok she will sink into the earth and return when the earth re-emerges from the cataclysm. From all this we can see that Idunn was a regenerative force, giving youth to the Æsir and fertility to humans (see Gna). This is probably why she survived Ragnarok; to distribute her apples to the new deities.

Her story appears in a text from about 900 CE, which calls Idunn the woman who knew the medicine of the gods.[44] Also, when Skirnir is presenting Freyr's proposal to Gerd, he tells her she will have the apples of the Æsir, so presumably everyone knew about their effect. People were also buried with them, perhaps in the hope of rebirth. The apple motif appeared also in Greek and Celtic mythology, as the fruit of the Hesperides or Blessed Isles. As for Idunn, she strongly resembles the Greek goddess Hebe, who was the cupbearer to the Olympians, serving them their ambrosia.

An obscure reference to Idunn's life appears in the *Lokasenna,* source of so much gossip about the deities. When she tried to make peace between Loki and her husband, Loki said:

> *"Be quiet, Idun!   You, of all women*
> * the one most mad for men:*
> *you have locked   your arms in love*
> * around your brother's bane."*
> (Terry)

So Idunn had a brother, whom Bragi must have killed. No other source mentions him.

Eír

The goddess of healing, she sat on the mountain Lyfja (Healing) and gave health to any woman who could climb it. She gathered medicinal herbs from all over the world to cure people. Snorri calls her "the best of doctors".

Saga

Most of what we know about the goddess of history comes from this stave:

> *Sokkvabekk called   is the fourth*
> * which cool waters ripple round about;*
> *there Othin and Saga   all their days drink,*
> * glad from gold cups.*
> (Hollander)

She is invoked for a good memory. She is sometimes thought to be the same as Frigg, but unlike her, Saga actually speaks of what she knows. Her name means "Seer", and in Indo-European myth, to see is connected to knowing, especially supernatural knowledge.

Sjofn

Her name means "love", so she is probably connected to Lofn and Vor. According to Snorri, "*she is much concerned to direct people's minds to love, both women and men.*" (Faulkes)

Var

She oversees the swearing and keeping of oaths. Her name, which is related to the word "beware", may be a caution against making rash oaths or breaking one's word. The promises that lovers made were enforced by her as well. (These contracts were called varar after her.[45]) She is mentioned in the *Thrymskvida* when Thrym and Thor exchange vows, so presumably she watched over marriage oaths as well.

Sif

Sif is Thor's wife, famous for her hair of gold. Loki cut it for a joke, which is interesting because that was a punishment if a woman had been unfaithful. The poem *Lokasenna*, which has Loki insulting all the deities, implies that he slept with her. In reparation, Loki got the dwarves to make hair of gold, which grew like real hair once it was attached. Ullr was called Sif's son, although Sturluson doesn't say if Thor was his father. She is a swan maiden as well.

According to the *Edda*, she was a seeress, and her kindred is unknown. Her name means "affinity, kinship by marriage" so she may have personified relationship in some way.

Nehellenia

This goddess has shrines in both German and Celtic territory, which show her with a basket of apples, a dog, and the prow of a ship. From these symbols scholars deduce that she protected seafarers, and had power over life (apples) and death (dogs are symbols of the underworld). She was especially revered in Frisian territory.

Fulla

Frigg's sister. Fulla carried her jewel-box, looked after her slippers, and shared her secrets. As a maiden, she kept her long hair loose, bound at the temples with a golden band. She and Frigg are invoked in a formula for a sprain. Under the name Abuntia, she survived into folklore. Women would leave pots in the larder open so that when she visited at night she could eat and drink. This guaranteed the prosperity of the house.[46]

Gna

Another of Frigg's servants, she was a messenger with a flying horse called Hooftosser. Her name was a synonym for "woman" and is derived from *ga-naha, "abundance".[47] This would seem to associate her with Fulla. When a husband and wife prayed to Frigg for children, she sent Gna to throw an apple into the man's lap, which his wife ate and thus conceived. Monaghan thinks she was a wind-goddess.

Hlín

She comforted the grief-stricken and gave them relief. She also provided refuge for people that Frigg let escape from some disaster. In some cases, like the *Völuspá*, it seems that Hlin is another name for Frigg. Hnoss Freya's daughter, whose name means "Treasure", and was a kenning for a jewel. She was the goddess of infatuation. In the *Skaldskasparmal* she is called "gold-wrapped" (Faulkes). Her sister's name was Gersemi, but nothing is known about her.

Lofn

She was a love-goddess who received the prayers of separated lovers, and brought together those she favoured. Her name means promise or permission, and she smoothed love's path for those who were not allowed to marry.

Rínò

Mother of Vali by Odin. He came to her because she was the woman who would bear Baldr's avenger. The first year he came as a soldier, but she refused him. The next year he came as a smith, and fared no better. The third time he cursed her with sickness, and came as a young maiden with healing powers. He cured her, and so got her to sleep with him.

Snotra

A goddess of wisdom, and one of the Asyniur. Her name meant "awareness", and she knew all that passed.

Syn

A goddess of doorways, she guarded the entrance to the doors of a hall against those who were not allowed there, and was a defence at assemblies against something they wished to refute. *"Thus there is a saying that a denial (syn) is made when one says no,"* according to the *Gylfaginning.* (Faulkes) Her name was a kenning for "woman".

Dísír

These grandmothers were the ancestral goddesses of a clan, who looked after its interests. Often they prophesied on the outcome of major events in family life. They had their own festival, the Disirblot. This appears to have been a woman's cult, and a group of women celebrating the festival were burnt in their house rather than convert to Christianity.

Nerthus

The goddess Tacitus described being paraded in the wagon (see Religious History) was named Nerthus. He identified her as Tellus Mater, the Roman earth-goddess, and so most writers have assumed she was also an earth-mother. Like Freyr, her travels in the wagon brought peace to the land, since weapons were taboo during her festival. Also, in both cases it was a general holiday, which was identified with peace and a good harvest.

The translation of her name is the subject of some disagreement: it comes from the Celtic word *nerthos* "force", it comes from a Proto-Indo-European root *ner-* which indicated male power, it is derived from the Greek *nerteroi*, "from the Underworld", virility, it is related to the Sanskrit word *nart*, "dancer", or it could come from Lithuanian, either from *nerti*, "to dive" or from *nerseti* "to play".

As one author points out, the idea of a goddess whose name means "virility" is not as odd as it might seem. The Hindu Durga and the Greek Artemis and Demeter have titles like "the strong, the forceful" or "the aggressive".[48] There is also the possibility of a feminine and masculine form, such as is found in the names Zeus- Dione, Hera-Heracles and Jupiter-Diana. Or, indeed, Norse pairs like Freyr-Freya and Fjorgyn-Fjorgynn. As Näsström says, the male part of the pair would be Njord. This would eliminate the idea that Njord was Nerthus after a sex-change, and solve the mystery of who his sister/wife was.

The downside of the cult was that the slaves who bathed the statue of Nerthus were drowned. This may account for some of the corpses found in the bogs of Denmark. These were mainly women and children, and some chariots and horses were found as well.[49]

Hel

The goddess of the afterworld was Hel, whose gloomy abode was named for her. Half of her face was black, the other dead-white. Her nine-ringed realm was a miserable place, even in Hel's hall, Sleet-Cold. There she was served by Senility and Dotage, and ate with a knife and fork called Famine from a plate called Hunger. Those who died of old age or disease went to her.

Nanna

Baldr's wife, and the daughter of Nep, a giant. She may have been a giantess herself, since her name was used as a kenning for them. She died of a broken heart when her husband was killed, and they went to Hel together. When Hermod visited them she sent a ring to Fulla and a linen robe and other gifts to Frigg, her stepmother. Her son was Forseti, the god of justice. Nanna's name was also used as a kenning for woman, which may mean that she was a more popular goddess than the written sources indicate.[50]

Oestre

The goddess of spring and dawn in Germany and England. The Venerable Bede says that a month was named for her and she was worshipped then. As a result, her name became the English word for the Paschal Festival: Easter.

Norns

The three goddesses of fate carved runes in Yggdrasil to affect destiny and create wyrd. Their names were indicative of their activities: Urd (fate), Verdandi (becoming), and Skuld (debt). They lived at the roots of Yggdrasil, sprinkling the tree each day with water from Urd's well. There were also personal norns who set individuals' fates at their births.

Gerð

This giantess lit up the world every morning: *"when she lifted her arms and opened the door for herself, light was shed from her arms over both sky and sea, and all the worlds were made bright by her"*. (Faulkes) Freyr saw her one morning and fell in love with her, so he sent his servant to her. Gerd was not interested in marrying any of the gods, however, so Freyr's servant began making runes, threatening her with ugliness and unsated lust, and so she gave in. However, she requested his horse and his sword, which is why Freyr fights at Ragnarok with a stag's antler. According to some sources, they had a son, Fjolnir, who became a king.

The way this myth is interpreted tells us a lot about how mythologists see women and goddesses. The most popular interpretation is that Freyr is the sky-and-sun-god, fertilising the wintry earth-goddess Gerd, whose name is glossed as "field" or "enclosure". Others have seen this myth as a ritual of marriage between the fertility god and the earth, to bring about fecundity in humans and animals, or a sky-god and earth-goddess mating.

There are several things wrong with these ideas. First, Gerd is a giantess, a group not normally associated with fertility. Freyr's conquest of her through his minion can be seen as a typical myth where the gods attempt to gain some boon or pull a trick on the giants, and succeed by guile or force.

Second, while Freyr is a god who promotes fertility, he is not a sky-god. The folklore of the Scandinavians does not show any signs of a sacred marriage between a sky-god and an earth-goddess.[51] Nor does the idea of the god as a sexual defroster appear anywhere. Thirdly, while there is an element of love about Freyr's attraction, the way that

Gerd is wooed makes the courtship a battle of wills, rather than a willing marriage between complementary partners, as an earth- sky marriage should be.

Another problem is that it is uncertain whether Freyr married her or just slept with her. There is nothing in *Skirnirsmal* to suggest that he married her, just that he met her in a grove and had sex with her. However, when Freyr became the patron god of the Swedish dynasty, his liaison with Gerd was legitimated so that the kings could claim legitimate descent from both a giantess and a god, just as those who claimed descent from Skadhi and Odin did.

Sol/Sunna

The Germanic sun-goddess, who rode through the sky each day in her chariot drawn by two horses, Alsvid (All-Strong) and Arvak (Early-Awake), carrying the shield Svalin (Cool) to protect the earth from being scorched. She was the daughter of the giant Mondilfare, who named her and her brother after the two sparks Sun and Moon. This angered the gods, who took the two children and set them to driving the chariots that carried the lights through the sky. She will drive her chariot until Ragnarok, when she will be eaten by the wolf Skoll, and when the earth rises anew her daughter will take up the job. Her power was that of warming and nurturing, the opposite to that of the frost giants, whom she turned to stone (along with dwarves, since they lived underground).

Bil

A girl stolen by Mani when she and her brother were sent to fetch water after dark. While both siblings now live with the moon, only she was deified. She was invoked by poets for inspiration.

Nott

She was the goddess of Night and a giantess, who rode through the sky with Mani the moon-god. Her horse was Frost-mane and his shaking his mane left hoar-frost on the earth. She had three husbands. The first was Naglfar (Twilight), by whom she had Space, the second was Annarr (Second) whose child was Jord, and her third Delling (Dawn), and that produced Day.

Jord

She is the Scandinavian earth-goddess, and Nott's daughter. She was said to be married to Odin, who was Thor's father, but this was probably a later part of her mythology. Jord was important enough to be numbered among the Asyniur.

Minor Goddesses

Ahrenkonigin: Austrian "queen of corn ears"

Hariasa: German war-goddess.

Harimela: German war-goddess.

Hertha: a Germanic earth-goddess. Ploughs were blessed in her name.

Hlodyn: Germanic "protector of the hearth"

Hrede: Bede mentions her as an Anglo-Saxon goddess. March was named after her.

Kornjunfer: German corn-goddess.

Perchta: a goddess of Germany, Austria and Switzerland. She gives fertility and keeps spinning-women up to the mark. Her holiday is the Feast of Epiphany.

Sjojungru: Scandinavian sea-goddess.

Sjora: Swedish sea-goddess.

Tamfana: a German goddess mentioned by Tacitus.

Ziza: (Cisa, Ciza) was honoured by Germans on Sept. 28.

General Comments

There is some confusion about the identity and myths of the various goddesses. Both Frigg and Freya have well-developed stories about necklaces, and Loki hints that Gefjon also traded intercourse for one. The similarities are intriguing. Patricia Monaghan suggests that the necklace was a solar attribute, and as Sól lost her earlier prominence, the other goddesses picked up her various emblems.[52] The female nature of the sun would have helped this process along. The small brass figure of a woman in a necklace and a skirt from the Bronze Age (mentioned in the Religious History chapter) may be connected to the various goddesses with necklaces. She has round eyes, a necklace, and cups her left nipple with her hand, all of which point to a solar cult (the breast was a sun-symbol for the Inuit and Aborigines of Australia).

Another problem is whether each goddess is separate or whether they are mainly hypostases of Frigg and Freya. There are many goddesses who appear in the court of Frigg, and so they are often assumed to be part of Frigg. Hlin in particular is listed in Snorri as a name of Frigg, so one can assume that the two are the same. Of course, as with Gefn and Freya, even if once the two goddesses were the same, this doesn't mean that they have to stay the same. While many scholars, especially the comparative mythology ones, see all the Norse goddesses as part of one Great Goddess whose main expressions are Frigg and Freya, I think that they all must have had at least some reality or why would they be mentioned separately? After all, the avatars of Vishnu, for example, are important in their own right, and no one would dream of confusing the three parts of the Christian Trinity. It is only when the figures in question are goddesses that they have to be reduced to some sort of common denominator.

Another common assumption, found alongside the idea of one Great Goddess, is that this goddess is necessarily an earth and fertility deity. The writers who follow the Dumézilian theory tend to fall down here, because they assume that the goddesses are one, their trifunctional goddess. But, if this goddess has power in the spheres of rulership and magic, battle and fertility, why is she then reduced to her fertility-aspect only? There are two reasons: first, the role of goddesses in Indo-European myth is still hazy, and second, fertility is supposed to be what women are good at, despite the evidence that the Norse associated fertility with males. I discuss some other reasons why goddesses tend to be associated with fertility rather than any other function in the Gender and Mythology chapter.

Gods

Odin

The head of the Germanic pantheon, husband of Frigg. He is the god of the runes; he hung himself on Yggdrasil for nine nights to get them. He is a god of magic, who inspires poets and berserkers. The root of his name is a word meaning furious or inspired. He leads the Wild Hunt and seems to have usurped Tyr's role as the Sky-Father. While he had numerous affairs, they always seem to involve elements of trickery, which suggests that the one-eyed Odin is not very sexually appealing.

Thor

The thunder-god, in outline he is like the guy in the Marvel comics. The difference is that he is red-headed, with a beard, and isn't helpless without his hammer. He is the god of the common people, while Odin was the aristocratic patron. They looked to him for protection, and he was one of the most worshipped gods. His role in myths is to kill harmful giants and perform feats of strength (including prodigious eating and drinking). Sif is his wife, and their two sons are Magni and Modhi.

Freyr

A fertility god, who was worshipped by a great many people. He was Freya's brother and lover, since brother-sister marriage was permitted among the Vanir. He was associated with the Light Elves and brought good weather and crops to farmers. He was also called on by warriors, probably in his boar shape.

Balðr

Frigg and Odin's son, who dies of a mistletoe dart. He is a rather mysterious character, whose main function is to die, and stay dead until Ragnarok. We know that he was beautiful and radiant, and perhaps his death preserves some of the good of Asgard for the next cycle of creation. He was married to Nanna, and their son was Forseti.

Heimðall

The watcher god, an essentially mysterious character whose origins are unknown. He is the son of nine sisters, and watches at the head of Bifrost, the rainbow bridge. When the final battle between the gods and giants begins, he will summon the Æsir with his horn.

Mani

The moon-god, Sól's brother. He stole the children Hjuki and Bil from earth because they were carrying water after dark. Mani is the god of the calendar; he controls the waxing and waning of the moon, and the Germans had a lunar calendar.

Loki

Loki was the trickster god, who got into trouble and embroiled the other gods with him. His mischief was originally constructive, since the deities got many treasures from his quick-witted solutions to problems. Eventually he got out of hand, and was bound under the earth with only his wife Signy standing by him. His children included Hel, the giantess Angerboda, the Fenris

Wolf and Odin's eight-legged horse Sleipnir (which he gave birth to in the shape of a mare).

Tyr

The god of fairness, justice and war. He was the original sky-father before being elbowed out by Odin. His war connection comes from the tradition of trial by combat, which he presided over just as he did regular trials and all judgements. His one spot of oathbreaking led to the loss of his right hand.

Bragi

As the exemplary poet, he was the patron of skalds. Idunn was his wife.

Njord

Sea-god, Freya's father. His children were conceived with his mysterious sister, whom Loki makes reference to (Nerthus?). He was also married to Skadhi, but was soon divorced again.

Ullr

God of winter, Skadhi's second husband. He lived in Ydalir (Yew-dale), and his symbols was the bow.

Forseti

Nanna and Baldr's son. He was the god of justice, symbolised by his double-edged axe.

Gender & Mythology

A feminist reader of Norse myth will see certain things as central issues, things that perhaps other people would not consider important, or even miss the significance of entirely. In this chapter I discuss several different topics of Norse myth as they related to gender. What I find is that in some ways the Norse were very sexist, which isn't very surprising, since for most of human history people have been very sexist. However, there are some bright spots, and I cover some of these.

Creation and gender

The creation myths discussed in the Origins chapter, which seem to involve only males, require a closer look. It seems peculiar to us that the Norse and Germans could have believed that no women were involved in creating the worlds. The standard explanation offered for this is that they were sexist, or covering up earlier myths, as the Greeks are often said to be doing. However, I think that it is our reading of these myths that needs questioning.

One general assumption often made about mythology is that women and goddesses symbolise fertility. The fact that it is women who carry the foetus and then give birth has been the basis of a bundle of ideas about life and its origins among both primitive and sophisticated cultures. Writers may be dismissive of these powers, or like the new feminist authors, celebrate them, but no one denies their association with women and the Great Mother

Goddess. Mircea Eliade's book *Patterns in Comparative Mythology* is a typical example, saying:

> *One of the first theophanies of the earth as such, and particularly of the earth as soil, was its "motherhood", its inexhaustible power of fruitfulness.*"[53]

What can be said, then, about a culture that does not appear to share this set of ideas? If a group of people do not appear particularly interested in female fertility, what does this say about them? One common answer is to assert that this is the result of a sexist cover-up. The males and gods have stolen the feminine powers, and therefore the women and goddesses have suffered a loss of power. While this is an understandable feeling, this sentiment is wrong. First, it assumes that other peoples have the same basic set of ideas we do, and are just covering up so that men can take over. Second, I feel that a lot of the discussion of the reverence for the Great Goddess who gives birth is motivated more by the lack of respect mothers get today than any desire to understand prehistoric culture. (Of course, as long as mythology has been studied, there have been people reading their own preoccupations into ancient myths, rites and artefacts. The next century may well be as amused by us as we are by the Victorians.)

There is also the fact that in terms of fertilising potential, men are much more fecund than women. Now that primitives are allowed enough intelligence to know where babies come from, I think it's safe to assume that they know this, too. Men can get women pregnant (in theory) every time they have sex, while women can only get pregnant for several days every month. This is very basic, and everyone knows it, but still women are seen as the fertile sex, and so women take the Pill, and women go to fertility clinics. (Imagine for a moment what it would be like if it were the other way around.) Among the Inuit, for example, the great Earth Mother doesn't make an appearance, because the earth isn't fertile, and the birth rate has to stay low.

Ronald Hutton recently questioned the whole idea of a Wiccan-style fertility goddess of earth and darkness during a conference at Ambleside. He pointed out that ancient goddesses: ...*presided over rulership, war, justice, handicrafts, poetry and many different aspects of the natural world including the Sun.*[54] In contrast, the modern concept of a goddess is of a Great Mother, which was developed by the Romantics and further embellished by 1950s conservatives like Jaquetta Hawkes. The unified concept of a single goddess has been under fire for some time now, and is probably a modern creation.

It is often used, however, by writers who can't explain the Norse goddesses any other way. Britt-Mari Näsström, for example, considers that all the goddesses listed in the *Gylfaginning* are parts of a Great Goddess who split into Freya and Frigg. She and other comparativists try this as a way of accounting for goddesses within the Dumézilian framework, since it only considers one goddess for its three or four gods. She accounts for the two goddesses' independent behaviour by conflating them into one Great Mother Goddess who is both mourning mother and lascivious love-deity.[55]

I can't help but feel that the idea that female equals fertility obscures the actual beliefs that the Bronze Age people had. In Gro Mandt's survey of Bronze Age rock art, she rather reductively assumes that the only type of female figures she can look for are associated with fecundity and sexuality. She considers the rock carvings to be a fertility cult, and when she finds many male figures she is puzzled. But then she points out that there are some votive offerings of feminine figures. Perhaps these are fertility goddesses?[56] The possibility of their being any other kind of goddess is simply ignored.

She suggests three explanations for why there is little sign of a fertility goddess in the rock art of an agricultural age and area. First, that the presiding deities are actually male, and not female. Second, that despite their non-presence, the female deities were necessary for fecundity. The sacred marriage scenes become important here. Third, that other symbols than the strictly genital or figurative represent the feminine spirit of fruitfulness. I will now look at these ideas, but leaving the first argument for last, since I see it as the solution to this particular question.

If female divinities were important for fertility, despite their lack of representation, then the few scenes that do show women (or what we assume are women) become very important. Chief among these are the "sacred marriage" scenes. These take place on boats or land, and show a male and a female facing each other. One of the problems with such pictures is that often the "female" merely looks like a stick figure in a Smurf hat, which is supposedly her long hair. Davidson interprets these scenes as a ritual marriage (or possibly sacred one-night-stands) designed to bring fertility, which is probably the source of this idea.

However, as Lotte Motz points out, there is no evidence that these pairings have anything to do with fertility.[57] The duo appear on a boat, or on their own, but never with plants around them or farmers, or anything else that would suggest an agricultural ritual. The whole sacred marriage idea is somewhat questionable anyway. There is no instance of any of the possible sky-gods (Odin, Tyr) being ritually wedded to the earth in any form, so where would this notion come from?

As for the second suggestion, that the earth-goddess is invisible, this idea has the beautiful property of being completely unprovable. If the goddess cannot be depicted, then no proof of her worship will exist. The exact same "proof" can imply that she does not exist. A slightly more powerful argument is that the goddess is shown indirectly, through various symbols. These include: boats, foot-prints, wagon, cup-marks, snakes, and the circled cross.

These marks can just as easily be interpreted as the signs of an early sun cult, since all these things can be related to the sun-goddess. Of course, this would still represent a feminine power, but not a fertility goddess. Other writers have interpreted them as indicating various male deities. Clearly there is no one reading of these symbols, since they don't come with labels. This makes it difficult to say that they are proof of an earth-mother cult.

As for the rock art images of women that can be found, Lotte Motz suggests that they fit into the same pattern as the Sheela-na-gigs of Ireland. The female figure with cup-mark between the legs is a warning symbol, which keeps off evil. Myths associated with these figures, such as Baubo in Greece and Thor's encounter with the giant's daughter, show that the exposed female genitals were feared and respected for their effects on the viewer, rather than any fertility connotations they had.[58]

So, if there are no clear-cut images of the fertile female earth, can images of a male deity of fecundity be found? If you look at the Bronze Age petroglyphs, the immediate thing that strikes you is the number of male figures with erect penises. Did men go about in a state of perpetual arousal back then? Or do they have another meaning? Some of them are even quite perverse, showing a priapic figure facing a cow or horse. My guess is that they are the fertility figures, representing the intuition that the male is the fecund sex.

The idea of a male fertility deity lends a certain constancy to Norse myth. The phallic figures that appear in the Bronze Age rock art just mentioned could be associated with the god Freyr, who was often depicted with a large, erect penis. The Swedes worshipped him for his ability to bring fertility, as well as his other abilities. He and his father/uncle Njord are two of the Vanir, who looked after the fruitfulness of earth and water. The Norse creation myth then becomes less of an anomaly and fits into a pattern whereby the ability to create life is seen as a masculine attribute.

Snorri Sturluson states explicitly that Freyr is a fertility deity:

> He is ruler of the rain and sunshine and thus of the produce of the earth. He also rules over the wealth of men. (Faulkes)

However, in the same paragraph he says of Freya:

"She is the most approachable one for people to pray to...[i]t is good to pray to her concerning love affairs". (Faulkes)

If she were indeed a goddess of crops or fecundity wouldn't he say so? Given the nature of the Vanir, it seems unlikely that if she did have a connection to fertility it would go unmentioned. What is more likely is that Freyr is the god who gives good harvests and ensures new life, while Freya is a goddess of love and wealth. (Her fabulous necklace, tears of gold and amber, and her two daughters named Treasure all point to her as a goddess of wealth.)

The fact that creation is a mainly male activity, along with the male Vanir's fecundating nature, suggests that the Norse did indeed see fertility as primarily male. And it is not wrong that they did so. Expecting the Norse to think as we do is to take them out of history and their own circumstances, and turn them into exemplars for today, which denies their own reality. It has the disadvantage of sidelining female abilities in this sphere, but it frees women from the burden of being the Great Earth Mother.

Sun and Moon

The gender of some things seems to be so natural that it goes without question that, say, the earth is female, the moon is female, and the sun is male. Once again, however, the Norse confound this. The written sources explicitly state that:

> "There was a person whose name was Mundilfaeri who had two children. They were so fair and beautiful that he called the one Moon and his daughter Sol [sun], and gave her in marriage to a person called Glen". (Faulkes)

Compare this to Tony Willis' assertion (in the *Runic Workbook*) that the sun and moon are actually male and female, and that to assume otherwise is to be misled by grammatical gender. He and writers like him seem to feel that the Norse writers didn't know their own myths.

Both the sun and moon have suffered from people who want to change their gender for various reasons. Lee Hollander's translation of the *Poetic Edda*, for example, "corrects" the genders of the sun and moon, so that the fifth stanza of the *Völupsá* reads:

From the south the sun,	*by the side of the moon,*
heaved his right hand	*over heaven's rim,*
the sun knew not	*what seat he had,*
the stars knew not	*what stead they held,*
the moon knew not	*what might she had.*
(Hollander)	

Whereas the version quoted in Faulkes' *Snorri's Edda* reads:

> *The sun did not know where her dwelling was. The moon did not know what power he had. The stars did not know where their places were.* (Faulkes)

These two translations obviously have different ideas about the gender of the sun and moon. Why is this?

Most of the passages relating to the sun indicate that the author thought of it as a feminine being. In the *Gylfaginning,* one of the speakers says:

> *And this also will seem amazing to you, that the sun will have begotten a daughter no less fair than she is, and she shall follow the paths of her mother...*(Faulkes)

The list of the goddesses in the *Gylfaginning* includes Sól, the sun- goddess, as one of the Asyniur. The *Skaldskaparmal,* which instructed poets, tells them that the sun is:

> *...daughter of Mundifaeri, sister of Moon, wife of Glen...* (Faulkes)

(This relation of the goddess to her family isn't sexist, but standard procedure in kennings for all deities. One passage calls Odin "Frigg's darling".) The passage that refers to the wolf that chases Sól calls the sun "she" and "her".

On the masculine side, there are several passages that seem to see the sun as a male. One of these occurs in *Grímnismál*, when Odin says:

> *Svalin is hight*   *the Sun before,*
> *a shield*   *from the shining god.*
> *Would smoke and smoulder*   *both sea and land,*
> *if from him*   *it should ever fall.*
> (Hollander)

Some of the references to the sun as Alfrodul, the "ray of the elves" are in the masculine gender in the *Prose Edda*. The reference to Alfrodul bearing a daughter is obviously inflected feminine, while others are in the masculine. The goddess Skadhi also seems to attract masculine inflections, and this may be due to grammatical gender rather than any transsexual tendencies on the goddesses' part. (So, in a sense Willis is right to say grammatical gender is beside the point, but there is more than just grammar to support the sun's femininity.) There seems to be a general trend to a feminine sun in the Norse, German and English mythologies. The Balts, Slavs, and Celts also had sun-goddesses, so perhaps the sun-goddess isn't so atypical after all.

The Norse sources imply that the moon is a man called Mani, the sun's brother.

> *Moon governs the journeying of the moon and decides the time of its waxing and waning. He took*

from the earth two children, known as Bil and Hjúki... "(Faulkes)

Despite this, some authors have tried to find a triple moon goddess of the Wiccan variety in the myths. After all, if the sun was a man, then the moon must be a woman.

This raises the question of why they have to be opposite genders. The Persians and Vedic Hindus had gods for both sun and moon, while in ancient Irish and Welsh, the words for both are feminine. There seems to be a perception that male and female are "opposite" and this must be reflected in symbolism. A good example of this appears in one book on Norse myth, which shows a very sharply rayed sun with a man curled inside, while the moon is rather watery, a woman lazing inside it, her curves echoing the moon's. The same ideology that insists that the sun and moon are "opposite" insists that the moon must be a goddess.

The simple fact is, that the Norse apparently personified the actual sun as a woman, and the moon as a man. It seems odd that some writers find this odd or threatening, but there are some explanations. They may have something invested in the idea of the moon as the expression of a feminine mode, which must then be attached to women, while the masculine mode they relate to the sun is equally taboo for women. Also, most of us are accustomed to the notion of Greek mythology as "the" perfect set of stories, so we naturally perceive any deviation from the Grecian pattern as unusual and probably inferior. Since both the idea that gender is innate and the idea that the Greeks were better than the Norse have been discarded, perhaps readers and writers can better appreciate the different values that the Norse had for moon and sun, male and female.

Marriage among the Aesir, Vanir and Giants

Who marries whom is one of the points about Norse mythology that anthropologists have done a lot to illuminate. By looking at the various races of Norse mythology as tribal groups, they have highlighted the meanings of marriage as exchange among groups. Briefly, the giantesses marry Æsir or Vanir men, and Vanir women marry Æsir men. There is no reciprocal flow of Æsir women to the giants and Vanir.

Notice the way that this works out in the myths. After the war of the Æsir and Vanir, the two groups exchange hostages, but while the Vanir send a wife to Odin, there is no woman sent to the Vanir. While Freya might go to Asgard, Frigg or Sif would never be sent to Vanaheim. Indeed, Freya was married before, to her brother Freyr, but the Æsir did not recognise such marriages, and presumably she was re-married to the head Ase. These two things suggest that the Æsir won the war between the two groups. If the Vanir had won, presumably the power to choose wives would have gone the other way.

Freya was a frequent pawn in marriage negotiations. Three different giants tried to marry her as well. The first time this happened was when the Æsir took advantage of this to bargain with a giant who offered to build a wall for Valhalla in return for Freya, the sun and the moon. When it looked like he and his horse were going to finish it on time, Loki had to trick him by seducing his horse in the shape of a mare.

Another such incident was when Thor's hammer was stolen by a giant, who would only return it if Freya married him. Loki tried to talk her into it, but Freya was not having any of this. Thor went disguised as the goddess, and killed the giant when he got his hammer back. Another giant came to Valhalla, and under the protection of being a guest, boasted that he would kill them all and take Freya and Sif for himself. Only Freya was brave enough to serve him ale until Thor returned. He and the giant agreed to single combat, with fatal results for the reckless giant.

This has to be the only case where the gods tried to give a goddess to the giants. Even though Freya was a Vanir, she still was Odin's wife. Perhaps they figured on getting her back later, and indeed in two cases out of three they didn't offer her in good faith. The *Völuspá* seems to say that this was one of the things the Æsir did that ended the Golden Age:

> *who had filled the air with evil speech, offered to a giant the goddess Freya?* (Terry)

When one considers that marriage negotiations would involve the transfers of property, the guarantee of family alliances in case of trouble, and both families' prestige, it is not surprising that lying or false promise would be taken very seriously indeed.

While Freya, Sif and Idunn were not eligible for giants' wives, the giantesses Gerd, Skadhi and Nanna were certainly able to marry gods. Unlike their male counterparts, it would even seem that these women were desirable. Of course, in terms of the exchange theory previously mentioned, the giantesses could certainly be married to the gods, as long as the gods didn't have to hand their women over.

In fact, the myth of how the Æsir lost Idunn is a perfect example of how this system worked. Loki was trapped by a giant, Thjazi, into bringing Idunn to him, which he did, by means of a trick. Since Idunn held the apples that kept the deities young, they began to age in her absence. Naturally, they tried to find out what had happened to her, and when they learned Loki had given her away, they demanded he get her back. Loki returned Idunn, and the Æsir killed Thjazi. Skadhi came to avenge him, and instead married the Vanir god Njord. (Marrying into the enemy's family was a way to end a feud.) So the giant was punished for aspiring to the goddess, but the giantess was given a god, although a lower-rank god, as compensation.

The story of Gefjon fits in here, because she transgressed the boundaries that these marriages set up. To get Zeeland, she slept with a giant, and had four sons who used their giant powers to plow the land for her. Her name and Idunn's were not often used in poetic kennings, and Mundal thinks that it was because they spent time with the giants, which made their purity suspect amongst the skalds.

Of course, in Idunn's case she was kidnapped by a giant, and later restored to Asgard. There is no hint in the story that anyone reproached her for this; she and Bragi stayed married. In a Roman myth, she might have done a Lucretia and killed herself to remove the "stain", but it appears that everyone was glad to have her and her youth-preserving apples back.

So it seems that for the goddesses, as for the gods, there was little penalty for going against the rules. Certainly Odin never expressed any remorse for tricking Gunnlod or other giant women he had intercourse with. All the same, liaisons with giants are rare amongst the goddesses. It would seem that the Æsir wanted to keep power for themselves, rather than spreading it around through marriage. This makes sense if the motive is considered; Odin and the other deities wanted to stave off their doom, and the world's, for as long as possible. To that end, they used the power of the giants, which they tapped through their sexual arrangements.

Giants, Elves and Dwarves

The giants, elves and dwarves of Norse myth may sound a bit too much like the characters of a role-playing game, but they are a real part of the nine worlds. (They became part of the fantasy/gaming world through the Tolkien books, which he based loosely on Norse myth.) When I was young, I thought that these creatures were strictly male, since I'd never heard of any females. However, the giants and elves both have many female members of their races. The dwarves are a little more complicated.

Giants

In most accounts of Norse myth, the giants are forces of winter or sterility, who steal away the goddesses who give light and fertility to the world. This ignores the femininity of many giants, who bring benefits to the world of the Æsir and humans. Many of the giantesses are primal forces who contribute to creation and the order of the universe. Even the primal person, Ymir, is a non-gendered giant, so it is equally accurate to describe Ymir as a giantess. Only the sexism of our language, which makes the masculine the universal, keeps us from seeing this.

There are many other primal forces represented by females. Night is a giantess who rides the sky at night along with the moon. She gave birth to Audr ("Wealth"),

Day, who rides the sky along with the sun, and Earth, whose elemental nature should be obvious. (Oddly, Day's father was the dwarf Delling, hardly the obvious choice for a giant's husband.) Ran, the personification of the sea, was married to another sea-giant, Ægir, and they had nine daughters, who were the waves. Bestla was the mother of the gods, while the giants come from Bergelmir and his wife, who must have been the first giants.

Three of the most important gods come from giantess ancestors: Tyr, Heimdall, and Odin. In the *Hymiskvida*, we learn that Tyr's grandmother was a giant, and his mother, whose nature is uncertain, is also married to one. This makes for some difficulty, because Tyr goes along with Thor, the giants' enemy, to steal his father's cauldron. While both his grandmother and mother greet him pleasantly and help him, Tyr's father or step-father (it is uncertain what the relation is) is noted for his unfriendliness. This story also continues the tradition of the ugliness of giants, describing Tyr's grandmother as having "*Swart heads she had a hundred times nine*" (Hollander).

Heimdall's connection to the giants is a little bit more fantastic. He is said to be the son of nine mothers, with perhaps Odin for his father. (Odin is said to be the father of all the gods, including Thor, although this probably is part of his increasing popularity rather than any real parenthood.) These women have been variously identified, as Aegir's daughters, the waves; or else that he lived nine lives, like a cat. The Aegir theory falls down on the fact that his mothers' names and those of Aegir's daughters are different. Perhaps because of his odd parents, his status was ambiguous. Some sources call him an Æseir, some a Vanir. If Odin was his father, he should be an Æseir, but perhaps his low-status mothers demoted him to a Vanir.

Odin, along with his brothers Vili and Vé, is the son of the giantess Bestla and Bor. This seems to have had an effect on Odin, for unlike Thor, he can get along with giants, and even has sex with some of the giantesses. Odin's relations with giantesses is an interesting part of his sexual life. He only gets the mead of inspiration after he lies with Gunnlod for three days. While it seems that she was willing enough, in many other cases he has to resort to charms to get the giantesses into his bed. By means of magic, he coerces Rind into having sex with him after all else fails. He also lured seven sisters into his bed, "with wily words". Some of his other relations with giantesses are clouded in mystery. Whether he had to work magic to get Skadhi or Jord to sleep with him is not known, but both had children by him.

Thor, on the other hand, was the traditional enemy of the giants. Many tales of his exploits ended with him swinging his hammer about in a mass slaughter of giants. This hostility was modified when it came to the giantesses, who seem to have had a love-hate relationship with Thor. Grid, who was Odin's wife, gave him a magical staff and gloves. He was intimate with a giantess named Jarnsaxa, who was the mother of his super-strong son Magni. (One of Aegir's daughters was called Jarnsaxa.) He gave Magni a supernatural horse, although Odin criticised him for rewarding the son of a giant.

He also had hostile encounters with giantesses, which was more in keeping with his nature. In a dispute with Odin, he said:

In Eastland was I and slew etins [giants]
wanton wenches   who warred on mountains:
(Hollander)

He slew Geirrødr's daughter Gjalp, by throwing a stone at her vagina. He was being carried away in the flood of a river, and nearly drowned. He realised that Gjalp was menstruating in the river to swell it, and so he killed her. (The Norse apparently saw rivers as the effluvia of earth, personified as Jord. Calling rivers after urine or blood was a poetic device.[59]) The interesting point here is that as well as trying to kill the god, Gjalp is expressing her contempt for him by urinating or bleeding on him. Once he got to her father's castle, he used Gjalp's pole to kill her sisters, who were trying to press him into the roof. Their actions were a nasty parody of submission; he was sitting on a chair with them under it. He reversed it on them, however, by pushing on the ceiling with his pole, so that the chair went down on them, and so they were prostrate forever.

Despite Thor's hostility and Odin's exploitation, some of the other gods had more mutual relations with the giantesses. Njord, Baldr, and Freyr all marry them, with mixed results. All three are younger gods, and two of them come from the outsider Vanir rather than the dominant Æsir. This may be why they can consider marrying into another race/species (depending on how one views the different groups in the myths).

Another significant point about these marriages is that two of them begin with the giantess feeling hostile about her future spouse. Skadhi only comes to Asgard because she wants to avenge her father, whom the Æsir killed. By way of compensation, they offer her Njord in marriage. This is a gender reversal, because usually one of two warring families would marry their daughter into the other family to make peace. She begins dressed in her full armour, a vengeful outsider, and finishes as "*bright bride of the gods*" (Faulkes). She embodies the erotic and warlike nature of the giants. They often had relations with the gods, and were perceived as sexually appealing. However, the underlying hostility between the two groups could erupt in conflicts like the ones between Thor and various giantesses. When Skadhi becomes one of the Æsir, she reconciles both these aspects with the power of the gods and goddesses.

Gerd, on the other hand, had to be forced into marriage with Freyr, who would seem like a good match to most people. It is interesting that while normally the giants were shown desiring what the gods have, and trying various stratagems to get it, Gerd refused it when it was offered to her. Skirnir had to curse her with ugliness, sterility and unsated lust, before she gave in. These would be the opposite of the gifts that the Van Freyr was able to bestow.

Nanna, on the other hand, was married to the most desirable of the gods. Baldr was a sought-after mate, since Skadhi tried for him as well. (Perhaps he was the male equivalent of Freya, whom the giants tried to marry several times.) Unfortunately, there was no myth that told us how they met and married. What they have told us was that she loved him enough to accompany him to Hel, dying of grief at the sight of his body. She, unlike Skadhi, was able to move into the ruling family and marry the man who would rule after Ragnarok, so it is a pity there isn't more information about her. Her name was a kenning for troll-wife in Snorri Sturluson's manual for poets, a reference to her giant nature, which usually wasn't mentioned.

These giantesses defy the stereotype of the ugly giant, since three different gods found them desirable enough to marry. Gerd, indeed, rouses Freyr to love-sickness by merely looking out a window. Skadhi is never explicitly called beautiful, but she is "shining" like the gods and elves, and presumably as comely as they are. Tyr's mother, unlike his ugly grandmother, is called "brow-white" and "all dight in gold". She is clearly meant to be a lovely giantess, suitable for a god's ancestor.

Other erotic giantesses appear in the heroic sagas, often giving practical aid to the hero as well as their love. The story *Helgaqvida Hjörvardzsonar* has a troll-woman helping the warrior Hedinn in battle.[60] Grettir of Grettirs saga was involved with Thorir's daughters, and a giantess, Fridr, interceded with her father to save her lover from his wrath. Brana of *Hálfdanar saga Brönufóstra* counselled her lover while they spent the winter in a cave, and gave him precious gifts when he returned to the human world. Other times the giantess is an ancestor; in one saga a king says he found it pleasant to beget children in a cave with a troll- woman.[61]

Giantesses often had magic powers, especially of foreknowledge and supernatural wisdom. The prophetess in the Völuspa may have been a giantess; in verse two she says

I call to mind   *the kin of etins*
which long ago   *did give me life.*
(Hollander)

Her power to know the wyrd of the worlds probably comes from being of one of the oldest races, the giants. The sisters Fenja and Menja, who have their own saga, the *Grottasongr*, are called "foreknowing". In the *Hyndluljoth* Freya goes to a giantess, Hyndla, when she needs to find out what Ottar's ancestry was.

The Norse worshipped some giantesses. Jarl Haakon built a shrine in southern Iceland to the giantess Thorgerdr Hölgabrudr and her sister Irpa, who helped him in battle.

It stood in a grove, with lots of gold and silver carvings. This richness testifies to the importance of her cult. According to *Skaldskaparmal, ...a king named Holgi, after whom Halogaland is named, was Thorgerd Holgabrud's father. Sacrifices were offered to them both, and Holgi's mound was raised with alternately a layer of gold or silver - this was the money offered in sacrifices...* (Faulkes) In one saga a suppliant lays an offering of silver before her statue, in the belief that if she favours his voyage she will give him a ring from her finger. She protects her favourite Haakon by appearing during a battle, causing a storm and shooting arrows from her fingertips. In *Njal's Saga*, she and her sister Irpa appear with Thor in his carriage.

Another giantess who was worshipped in Norway was Gói. She was the daughter of Thorri, but another giant called Hrólfr kidnapped her and married her. Her family searched for her, and her father established a festival to her memory, but when they found her she chose to stay with her husband. Many of their descendants were kings of Norway. The Gói-blot is a festival on the order of Imbolc or Candlemas, since Gói means "February". Her father's festival is in January, which is also named after him.[62] She is a goddess in the mould of Frau Perchta and Frau Gode. There is more about these three in the Women's Mysteries chapter.

A memorial stone found in Hynnestand, in Sweden, shows a single female figure riding a wolf, using snakes as a bridle. This probably represents Hyrrokkin, the giantess who pushed out Baldr's funeral boat when no one else could.[63] She may have featured in funeral rites, since she was important enough to be depicted in stone. The Swedes worshipped Skadhi, as we know indirectly from place-names, but also from her words to Loki, that cold counsels would always come from her groves and shrines.

Several giantesses have names relating to holiness: Helga ("to sanctify, bless"), Hörgatroll (hörgr, "heathen altar"), Fjölvör, Leirvör, Sívör, Svivör, Skjaldvör (after the goddess Vör). A number of them have the element -dis ("goddess") in their names: Bergdis, Eydis, Glámdis, Skjalddis, Thórdis. These last were worshipped in North Germany with sacrifices, and aided heroes in their missions.[64] All of them probably received worship, or were considered holy.

Elves

In the *Völuspá*, there is a constant refrain, "*what of the Æsir, what of the elves?*" It might be more useful to ask, what are the elves? Lotte Motz once identified seven different kinds in a paper. Even the two main kinds, as identified by Sturluson, are still subjects of hot debate. Are they entirely different, or somewhat alike, or the same?

On the surface, these two main kinds of elves could not be more unlike: "*There is one place called Alfheim. There lives the folk called the light-elves, but dark-elves live down in the ground, and they are unlike them in appearance and even more unlike them in nature. Light-elves are fairer than the sun to look at, but dark elves are blacker than pitch.*" (Faulkes) The elves are defined in this by a series of oppositions: light-dark, beautiful-ugly, heavenly-earthy.

Before looking more closely at just how similar or different the light and dark elves are, let's look at their particular characteristics. The light-elves were traditionally beautiful, with words like the Old English *ælfsciene* ("elf-bright") testifying to the general agreement among the Germanic-speaking peoples that the elves were bright and fair. Skirnir ("Shining") was a typical elf, dwelling with the god Freyr in the sky. In fact, the actual home of the elves, Alfheim, was near Asgard, and the elves and sky-gods were often mentioned together. Dark-elves, on the other hand, are very similar to dwarves, being ugly, dark, and dwelling in the ground.

The light-elves were close to the Æsir, as the *Eddas* testify. The *Völuspá* links them, as well as *Grmnismál*, *Hávamál*, and many others. In the Skírnismal, Freyr complained that the Æsir and alfs will not let him have his love. The closeness of the two is emphasised in the *Lokasenna*, when the deities gather with the elves for a banquet in Ægir's home. Even an Old English charm links them together, so this must have been a fairly universal notion in the Germanic world.[65]

Freyr and Sól are particularly close to the light-elves. Freyr is the lord of Alfheim, which was given to him as a teething-gift. Like the elves he is a radiantly beautiful being, who is sometimes called skirr (shining). His assistant was called Skirnir, from the same word. As for Sól, she and the light-elves share the quality of brightness, and the word alf may come from the proto-Indo-European *albh, "whiteness, glow"[66]. Not only do the elves have their own name for the sun, but the name Alfrodul (Beam of the elves), is used several times in the Eddas to refer to her.

The dark-elves are not closely associated with deities. In fact, most of them seem to have shunned the dark-elves, just as they did the dwarves. However, Freyr and Sól can be shown to have a fittingly subterranean connection to them. Freyr was also the god of fertility, and some barrows were named for him. His avatar, the Norwegian king Frohdi, was buried in a barrow, rather than burned, to maintain the peace and plenty of his reign. Elves were also associated with barrows, and people apparently made sacrifices to them there. Some dead people in barrows, who were thought to be still living in some sense, and capable of giving boons, were also called elves. The connection between all of these is that Freyr is a primal ancestor, the "elves" in the barrows were ancestors, and they, along with the elves, were associated with barrows.

The sun's connection to the dark-elves involves a look at the dark side of the sun. The sun rose in the morning, rode her chariot across the sky, and descended in the evening. As a result, like many other sun-deities, she was assumed to be as potent in the underworld as in the sky. In a rather mysterious passage of the *Forspjallsljod*, the gods send messengers to the underworld during a terrible winter to address Gjöll's Sunna. This character seems to be an underworld sun, perhaps the sun in winter, since Gjöll ("Echoing") is the river that runs through the underworld. Other sun-goddesses, such as the Hittite Wurusemu and the Canaanite Shapash, also had power in the underworld.

The sacrifice to the elves mentioned previously seems to be closer to the world of the dark-elves than Alfheim. This was the alf-blot, which people celebrated in the fall. Unfortunately, we don't know very much about it. What we do know comes from two sources. In the *Yngling Saga*, a poet sought shelter in several farms, but no one would let him in. One woman came to her doorway, and told him that they were sacrificing to the elves:

> "Wreak his wrath will Othin,
> wretch," said a witchlike gammer.
> "Keep out," quoth she, "nor further
> come; for we are heathen."
> "Also," this ancient beldame

added, she who forbade me
foot to set in, the slattern,
"sacred to the elves we are making."[67]

Perhaps women made this offering, but there is no way to know.

This ritual was probably a household version of the sacrifice in *Kormák's Saga.* In that story, the wise woman Thordis sends a wounded man to: a mound not far from here, in which dwell elves; *"take the bull which Kormák slew, and redden the outside of the hill with bull's blood, and make the elves a feast with the flesh; and you will be healed".*[68] The later custom of leaving milk and some honey for the elves may be a less expensive version of this sacrifice. The word blot implies a sacrifice, so there must have been some sort of dead animal offered to the elves. Davidson thinks that the cup-marks found on stones may have been intended for the elves in their guise as earth-spirits. In Sweden people used to pour milk and other liquids in them, so maybe the two customs existed side by side. Milk and honey sounds like the kind of offering one would put in a cup-mark, whereas the animal sacrifice would be more appropriate to a household feast.

These marks are often found near sun-wheels, and I think that they point towards both a belief in rebirth, and also the association between the elves and the sun. According to Davidson, the cup-marks and the elves were connected with the dead, especially those who continued to influence affairs or guarded treasure in their graves.[69] Myths and grave practices connected the sun-goddess to the dead, as well. The images of suns in boats in prehistoric art come from the idea that the sun travelled from east to west during the day, and had to sail back to the east at night. People linked this journey to the travelling dead soul, burying people at dusk, or facing west, so that the sun would carry them along on her trip through the underworld at night.

The dualistic nature of the elves is not so mysterious after all; like Freyr and Sól, they had dominion in heaven and on earth. The differing forms of the dark and light elves may have been a result of a perception that just as things have different names in the various worlds, they may look different as well. Or it may be that the dark-elves and dwarves were conflated to the point that people began thinking they were the same.

On the level of folklore, there are other kinds of elves, including the exclusively female elves who appear to human men. Elf-women may very well be a borrowing from French and Celtic tradition, since they conform to the model of the desirable fairy-woman who appears, grants a boon and disappears. One such woman appeared in the form of a hart to the hero Hrolf, who followed her into the forest, and helped her deliver her child. For this good deed, he received many boons. (This incident connects with the instruction of Sigurth in the *Sigrdrífumál*, where the Valkyrie Sigrdrífa taught him birth-runes, as well as more warrior-like magic.) King Helgi helped a beggar dying of cold, who asked him to share his bed with her. When he did, she turned into a beautiful woman, and later bore him a child. In the *Yngling Saga*, one of the characters was Alfhild, an elf-woman, whose father and grandfather were rulers of Alfheim. She married King Guthröth, and their son was Olaf.

Further evidence of the importance of elves comes from the fact that people named themselves for them, just as they did with the names of the gods. There are many women in the various sagas who are named for the elves. There was also a historical woman, the mother of King

Magnus of Norway, who was called Alfhildr. Snorri Sturluson mentions her in *Saint Olaf's Saga*. She was the handmaiden to King Olaf, but he got her pregnant. She gave birth to the future King Magnus.

Dwarves

Terry Pratchett said in one of his Discworld books that even for other dwarves, it is impossible to tell the gender of dwarves. It follows, he said, that the courtship of dwarves is a very tactful affair. In Norse myth, there are no female dwarves, so there isn't much courtship at all.[70] What intercourse there is between the dwarves and goddesses or women has to be bought by the wonderful items the dwarves can make.

Even the origin of the dwarves is asexual. According to the *Gylfaginning*, they were born in the body of Ymir as maggots, but the gods gave them intelligence and humanoid form. The passage goes on to say that there are dwarves that come from rocks and ones that come from the soil. The *Völuspá*, however, suggests another origin. Verse nine says that they were made from the blood of Brimir and the limbs or bones of Bláinn.

The dwarves did not have women among their own kind, nor did they hold much attraction for the women of other races. The only person on record as marrying a dwarf is the giantess Nott, who married Delling. The dwarves did manage to get Freya to have sex with them, however. This came about because of their extraordinary skill in metalworking, which was the source of many gifts to the Æsir. The goddess was tempted by a magical necklace, and its price was a night with each of the four dwarves that made it. Part of the interest of this story comes from the contrast between the beauty of the goddess and the ugliness of the dwarves, and Lotte Motz compares it to the marriage of Hephestios and Aphrodite.

The dwarves shared this lack of physical beauty with the dark-elves, and the *Eddas* don't really distinguish between the two. Some of the dwarves in the *Völupsá* are called Alfr, Gandalfr, and Vindalfr, names which should belong to elves.[71] Both groups construct magical objects for the Æsir: the elves created Sif's golden hair, Thor's hammer and the Odin's magical gold ring, while the dwarves made Freya's golden boar and the palace of Menglod, which paralysed anyone who shouldn't enter. Like the dark-elves, dwarves lived in the ground, specifically rocks and mountains in the dwarves' case.

As a corollary to this ability to make things, dwarves in some sense sustain the universe. Four dwarves named for the directions hold up the sky. Another one, Thjodrorir, does this in a more magical way:

I know a fifteenth   that the dwarf Thjodrorir
  chanted at Delling's door;
power to the Æsir,   triumph to the elves,
  understanding to Odin.
(Terry)

By this rune, chanted at the dawn (Delling's door) the cosmic order was sustained. In the Catalogue of Dwarves, which appears in the *Völuspá*, it says:"*molded many manlike bodies the dwarfs under earth, as Durin bid them*" (Hollander).The dwarves made the first humans in this version of creation, which would make sense in light of their craftsmanship.

Dwarves were supposed to be omniscient as well as magically skilled. The *Alvissmal* was obviously intended to teach the lore of names, and the author clearly felt that a dwarf would know all the names for things. Alviss knows the names of the gods, humans, giants, elves and dwarves use for things like earth, sky, moon, etc. Thor began each question by saying that Alviss should know *"all that has ever happened"* (Terry). The dwarves also brewed the mead of inspiration from the blood of Kvasir, and this was so precious Odin stole it. Dvalinn and Dáinn are two dwarves who taught lore to the dwarves and elves respectively.

Women in Norse Society

A better housewife
will never come
to Hassmyra
to run the farm.[72]

(from a memorial stone, raised by a farmer for his wife, in Sweden)

The history of women is a subject that has suffered from a great deal of neglect. Considering the sexist nature of our society, that is hardly surprising. However, the explosion of feminist scholarship is changing this situation, despite the limitations of working with documents written by men for men. Occasionally one finds a record left by a woman, or which deals with women's interests, and this is invaluable.

Women's work has been traditionally divided into two categories, the private and the public. Work done in the home very often left no trace at all. It was not taxed, nor did poets write about it. Most of the evidence related to housewives will have to be archaeological. Women who moved into the public sphere, on the other hand, are easy to find, if only by their rarity. By doing things that only men were supposed to do, they became so singular that chroniclers put them in their histories. Of course, the chroniclers also made their disapproval of these women clear; Saxo Grammaticus takes a special relish in the defeat of warrior women.

Queens and kings

Queens are visible symbols of female power. As such, they have been both revered and loathed by those who wrote about them. Their role seems to have been that of an adviser and diplomat, who smoothed situations and offered advice to the king. Occasionally, however, they acted on their own, and this tended to rouse strong emotions in those around them.

Gunnhildr of Norway, for example, was apparently universally hated. *Njals Saga*, *Laxadaela Saga*, and *Egils Saga* revile her. But was she a truly evil woman, or just a victim of politics? Her husband, Eirikr Bloodaxe, eventually lost a struggle for the throne of Norway, and naturally the winner was also thought to be the better man. According to *Egils Saga* she tried to poison Egil, a skald and magician, worked seithr against him, and apparently tried to keep him from composing a poem to end the king's wrath against him by changing herself to a sparrow and chattering at him. In the *Laxdaela Saga*, she also worked a spell on Hrut, which *Njals Saga* says was to separate him and his first wife. *Laxdaela Saga* implies that she also granted her favour to Hrut's nephew, Olaf.

In most commentaries, the writers say that she was a nymphomaniac, but she slept with Hrut and Olaf after her husband had died. There is no record of her having affairs while married to Eirikr, and she had a poem written about him after his death, describing his entry into Valhalla. That seems like the action of a loyal wife, securing her husband's reputation. She certainly seems strong-willed, since she freely spoke her mind in public while her husband gave judgement, and she dominated her son. Perhaps the truest comment on her character was voiced by Ozur when she called him to court:

The moment we refuse her invitation, she will hound us out of the country and seize all we own, but if we accept, she will treat us as handsomely as she has promised.

Perhaps it was her strong will and great power for good or ill that attracted so much calumny to her name.

The power-struggle between Magnus Olavson and Svein Canuteson in about 1035 CE also featured several independent women. Svein's mother, Algiva, was with him as he ruled Denmark, and came in for her share of criticism during his rather unpopular reign. Since he was a minor, she was the real ruler, as regent. They tried to rule Norway with Danish law, which seems to have involved heavy taxation. The former king, now St. Olav, was becoming known for holiness, and Algiva also offended by refusing to see him as a saint. She tried to discredit the preservation of his body and the fact that his hair didn't burn, but opinion was against her, and thus her unpopularity increased. Algiva (or Ælfgifu in English) was Canute's concubine, and concerned that her sons get some legacy from their father.

On the other side were Magnus Olavson and his step-mother, Astrid. After Olav died, she had gone back to Sweden, and Magnus into exile in Russia. When he decided to try to reclaim the throne of Norway, he went to her for support. His mother had been Olav's concubine, but Astrid still came to his aid, and rallied support for her step-son. A skald called Sigvatr composed a poem in her praise for her actions:

Highly with our vows
For rich gifts we will pay.
The daughter of Olav
Whom Digre King had

A numerous host of Swedes
Held a thing out on Hangrar,
At that time when in the east
Astrid spoke for Olav's son.

She could not have given
The good Swedes better counsel
Even if the very manly
Magnus was her son.
Next after mighty Christ
She most brought it about
That Magnus might embrace
The whole of Harald's kingdom.

The mild Magnus may thank
Astrid for such mighty help:
The friend of the men left it
In her hands; it gladdened us;
The wise-woman has thus
Helped her step-son with counsel,
As few others did: the truth
I tell to her honour.
(Monsen/Smith)

Astrid managed to persuade the Swedes to back Magnus against Svein, and they did so in such numbers that Svein's men gave up when he saw them coming. Magnus then became king over Norway.

The essential tie between these women and the counter-example of Gunnhild is that all three try to affect the policy of kings and lords in their various ways. Gunnhild attracted hostility for her attempts to horn in on the feud between King Eirikr and Egil, which she did in a most practical way. The other two worked through more acceptable channels, both working for the patrimony and therefore as proxies for their sons. Gunnhild also claimed to want to support her husband, which shows that there was a thin line between acceptable aggressiveness on behalf of the family and what was perceived as self-seeking.

Michael J. Enright's paper "*Lady with a Mead-Cup*" also discusses the power of the queen or noblewoman with regard to the family line and supporting the power of the king. He sees the ceremony of serving guests with the mead-cup or horn as the major symbol of the queen's power. First, she served the king, naming him as king as she did so, which served the purpose of establishing his authority. (The same naming was part of the investiture ceremony when the king took the throne.) Then she passed the cup or horn around the hall, so that the order of precedence was established, and it would be quite clear what everyone's place in that order was. As he points out, many quarrels in Icelandic sagas began over questions of precedence. Since the feast was a communal bonding rite, the queen's part was an important one, establishing rank and setting a tone of welcoming formality.[73]

This ritual makes sense of the many times that goddesses offered drink to those who threaten the order of Asgard. When Freya served a giant or Sif gave Loki a cup during his insults in the *Lokasenna* they are attempting to restore order and being the good cop to Thor's bad cop, who will restore order forcefully if needed.

Notice also, that the Valkyries served mead to the heroes who went to Valhalla. A noblewoman who served out drink was following some powerful mythic examples. It was not just flattery when women were called "peace-weavers" for they smoothed over the jealousies and rivalries among the followers of a king or noble, behaving as diplomats of the court.

Battle-maidens

The popular image of a Norse woman is that of the Valkyrie: an armoured female with a sword. It is both true and not true that women fought in battles. The majority of Norse women never saw a battle, and certainly were not Vikings. There were, however, exceptions to this, and they deserve a closer look.

According to Saxo Grammaticus, women fought at the battle between Harald Wartooth and his Swedish nephew Ring. Hetha and Vebiorg led companies of men for the Danes. Saxo described them as women whose "*female bodies Nature had endowed with manly courage*". Hetha brought a hundred men. Of Visna, another Danish warband leader, Saxo said Visna was a woman hard through and through and a highly expert warrior. Her chief followers among the band of Slavs who thronged around her are known to have been Barri and Gnizli. Not only were these strong women, but men were willing to be led by them. Hetha led the right flank in battle, and Visna was the standard-bearer. Visna lost her right hand in the battle, and Vebiorg was killed, although she also killed one of Ring's men.

Afterward, the Danes asked Ring to put their land under Hetha, but Ring split the land up, and Hetha was given part of it to control. The men of Sjælland refused to be governed by a woman, so they begged the other leader, Oli, to take over. He agreed, and: after ordering Hetha to come to him, he forced her to withdraw her jurisdiction from all areas except Jutland, employing threats in preference to force; Jutland itself he made a tributary state, to ensure that a woman was not given a free hand over the realm. The men of Sjælland lived to regret this; Oli was a cruel leader and they eventually rebelled against him.

Saxo Grammaticus mentions some other warrior women in his narrative, with obvious disapproval.

Rusila seemed to have been in the narrative mainly so that she can be defeated; every time Saxo mentions her he also tells us how some man defeated her. Not only does her compare her to the Amazons, but, like them, she has to be defeated by a hero to show his manhood. She appeared several times in the narrative, always in the guise of a warrior-maid.

We learn that she fought Hvirvil, who defeated her and allied himself with her five confederates (Rusila may be the same woman as the historical "Red Maiden", who attacked Munster in Ireland.)

The main story of her life is the conflict between her and her brother for the Norwegian throne. This story appears in two versions: in one King Harald of Sweden goes to the aid of her brother Olaf, and he defeats her and another woman, Stickla. In another she declared war on all who supported the Danes, and won a battle against her brother's supporters. Unfortunately, she lost the next, against some Danish lords, and had to retreat. She encountered her brother's army while in retreat, and defeated him. When the king of all Denmark sent his full army and navy against her, the people ejected her and she was eventually hunted down and cut into pieces by her brother. Two of her followers, who had been pirating in Ireland, returned to avenge her, but lost single-combat fights against the king's champions.

Stickla's career began when Frothi of Sweden invaded her part of Norway. All the people there fled, and Saxo traces her desire for war to this: In order to preserve her chastity the girl Stickla stole away from her fatherland, preferring the sphere of war to that of marriage. She appeared again in company with Rusila, as one of the maidens Harald defeated. Stiklastad in Trondheimsfjord may have been named for her.[74]

Another warrior woman in Saxo's narrative was Alvild, who took to arms and became a pirate. She had many women with her, and a group of pirates took them for their leaders. Alvild eventually met her match in a former suitor, Alf, and they were married. Saxo goes into a digression then to explain that women did, in earlier days, fight in wars and use weapons. Alvild's daughter, Gurith, also "*put toughness before allure*" and "*spent every minute cultivating soldier's skills*".[75] When, after a devastating war, she discovered that no man of royal class could be found to marry her, she vowed chastity rather than marry a lower-class man. She learned warrior skills, and chose a bodyguard to protect her. She was later betrothed against her will to a Saxon noble, but a better suitor, who had left her to win glory, returned and killed the Saxon (and most of the guests) just in time.

An unrelated woman, who also had vowed chastity, was Lathgertha. She was one of many women in Norway who became a warrior after the Swedes killed their king. The Swedish king Frø had taken the Norwegian noblewomen to a brothel, to humiliate them. So when the hero Regner arrived, they donned armour and followed him, along with many other noblewomen who had been raped or feared they would be. Regner killed Frø, thus avenging his grandfather, the Norwegian king.

He then made enquiries about Lathgertha, whose valour had won him the battle, as he acknowledged. She only pretended to be interested in his wooing, and put a bear and hound on her porch, apparently to test him. After Regner killed the animals, she married him. He later divorced his wife, saying that she had once turned wild animals against him. (He had fallen for another woman.) Lathgertha later fought on his side against the Scanians, rallying the frightened troops by panicking the enemy. After the battle she killed her husband with a dart in his throat, and so became sole ruler. (Her new husband's name was not given.) Some writers think that Lathgertha may have been a valkyrie, since the text says that she flew, rather than ran around the rear of the enemy line. Others suggest that she was a minor goddess like Thorgerdr Hölgabrudr, who protected Jarl Haakon by firing arrows at his opponents during a battle.

While Lathgertha may seem a bit mythical, some other women who fought are much more well-attested. The Red Maiden who terrorised the Irish as a Viking leader was mentioned in the Irish chronicles. Another possible warrior is Princess Olga, who appeared in the Russian Primary Chronicle. She was either Slav or Scandinavian, and if she was a Viking she gave the name Olga (Helga) to the Russian language.[76] She was more of a commander than an actual warrior, but she fought in several battles and showed a keen sense of strategy. After Prince Igor died, the Derevlilans tried to marry her to Prince Mal, but she managed to outwit them. First she had their envoys killed in various creative ways (buried alive, burned in a bathhouse) then she got more of them drunk at her husband's funeral, and her followers killed them. After that, there was a war, which she won. She then restored order to Russia and ruled until her son's majority.

Skaldíc women

Although skalds (poets) tended to be men, who wrote long poems about war, there are some women who wrote or spoke verses as well. The skaldic art was an advanced one, using convoluted terms for everyday objects, persons and gods. For example, according to the *Skaldskaparmal*, *"A woman shall be referred to by all female adornments, gold and jewels, ale or wine or other drink that she serves or gives, also by ale-vessels and by all those things that it is proper for her to do or provide."* (Faulkes) Women could also be referred to by the word "goddess", or by a reference to one of the trees with feminine-inflected names.

There are two recorded instances of women who were known for their writing of skaldic verse. The first of these was Jórunn, called the "Skald-maiden". The *Heimskringla* mentions her as making a verse on the settlement between Eirikr and Haraldr Halvdan:

> *Halvdan (I know) had heard*
> *Of Harald Fairhair's*
> *Hard mood and it seemed*
> *That his future was black.*
> (Monsen/Smith)

This verse (Judith Jesch quotes it in full) commemorated the first quarrelling between the two kings, during the reign of their father, Harald Fairhair. Its witty summation of a political situation ensured its survival. Unusually for skaldic poetry, it commemorated two kings not going to war, and the verses depend for their effect on this irony.

Another woman who was a poet was Steinunn, the mother of the poet of Refr Gestsson. She made two verses which make fun of a German missionary whose ship sank, and compared Christ's power to save his people from shipwreck with Thor's:

> *Thor altered the course of Thangbrand's*
> *long horse of Thvinnill [ship], he tossed and*
> *bashed the plank of the prow and smashed*

it all down on the solid ground;
the ski of the ground of Atall [ship]
won't be buoyant on the sea
since the baleful gale caused by him
splintered it all to kindling.

The killer of ogresses' kin [Thor]
pulverised fully the mew-perch
bison [sea-ship] of the bell's guardian [priest]
(the gods chased the steed of the strand [ship]);
Christ cared not for sea-shingle
stepper [ship] when cargo-boat crumbled;
I think that God hardly guarded
the reindeer of Gylfi [ship] at all.[77]
(Jesch)

From these verses we can see that Steinnun knew the usual kennings, since she used so many phrases for a ship. She also uses irony, since poems about voyages usually praised the sailors and presented them as heroic, not failures.

One of the women credited with verses is Gunnhildr, who was the wife of Eirik Bloodaxe. He was the king of Norway who was king of York during his exile from his country. This king and queen are mainly known from *Egils Saga,* which details the feud between the sorcerer Egil and Gunnhildr. (This saga, along with *Njals saga* and *Laxadaela saga,* paint a very unflattering picture of Gunnhildr as a witch consumed by lust.) Her interest in poetry had her commission a poet to write the *Eiriksmal,* which has Odin welcoming her dead husband, and is definitely propaganda for her cause.[78]

She was credited with a verse herself, although it seems an unlikely one for her to say:

Hákon rode plank-horse [ship] onto
the back of the waves from the west;
the king let the prow bite the surf
and the prince has reached the fjords.[79]

She spoke this as a prophecy, after Eiríkr's rival Hákon was supposed lost at sea. It seems an odd verse because she called her husband's rival "king", so it may be that she never said it at all.

Another feminine use of verse for politics was that of Hildr Hrólfsdóttir, who threatened King Haraldr after he exiled her son. In the *Heimskringla*, her words to the king were recorded, although in the rather odd context of a mother pleading for her son. She said:

The name of Nevja is torn;
Now driven in flight from the land
Is the warrior's bold kinsman.
Why be so hard, my lord?
Evil it is by such a wolf,
Noble prince, to be bitten;
He will not spare the flock
If he is driven to the woods.
(Monsen/Smith)

It sounds more like a threat than a plea, pointing out the damage the angry Hrolf could do, and advising the king that the warrior's energy would be better used in his service than turned against the kingdom.

Working women

Once a woman was married, she essentially ran the household, with little or no interference from her husband. When men were away on Viking raids, they had to run them by themselves. On larger farms there was more of a division of labour between men and women, but on small holdings women often did even the heaviest sorts of labour. Farm work was as much supervision as anything else, since women looked after all the production that went on, of food, clothes and other handiwork. In Icelandic law, this was the only job they were allowed to have. Despite this, they couldn't represent the farm in public business, although if they were the head of household, they were still taxed like a man was. The proportion of farms named after women (and thus probably owned by women) was ten times greater in Iceland than Norway, so perhaps women still had a better deal there than in the rest of Scandinavia.[80]

This was probably because Iceland was a new colony, so women could get some land in a new area, rather than trying to disrupt land-ownership patterns in settled areas. Iceland's laws made provision for a woman to claim land, stating that a woman could have as much land as she could lead a two-year-old heifer around in one spring day.[81] By contrast, a man was allowed a band of followers to help him carry fire around the boundaries of the property he wanted. Land-ownership was the mark of wealth in the dark and medieval periods, and was a method of buying loyalty. Aud the Deep-Minded managed to keep her followers loyal by giving them shares of her land in Iceland.

Women who went with the Vikings to England also managed to get land for themselves. Since women were able to own property in their own names, their possession of land was recorded in the *Domesday Book* and other English documents. Raventhorpe, a town name in both Lancashire and Yorkshire, was derived from the Norse name Ragnildr, as earlier spellings (Rageneltorp, Ragheneltorp) show. In the Yorkshire Raventhorpe a woman named Gida (Gytha) held four hides and five manors along with three men, and she also had a manor in Leckonfield. A woman named Ingrede (Ingiridr) owned a manor in Hotham, Yorkshire, along with her husband, Grim. Another woman called Sigrede (Sigirithr) also had two properties: a hide in Sutton, and a manor at Watlas.[82] Presumably these women also administered the properties they owned, just as a male landowner would.

Apart from managing a farm or owning land, women had a range of other employments. Most of these came about with the rise of towns in the twelfth and thirteenth centuries, since the farmers tended to be quite self-sufficient, needing very little from outsiders. Once people started living in cities and towns, there became more of a market for services and ready-made goods, as well as opportunities for importers to sell their merchandise. Oddly, one of the best ways for a woman to get involved in a business was either to marry someone already in it, or to inherit it from her family.

Women probably took advantage of these opportunities: in the merchant town of Birka, women's graves sometimes held weights and balances, which suggests that they might have been traders or merchants. Other women financed ships that went abroad on business, and took a cut of the proceeds. (The *Groenlendinga Saga* records how Freydis went halves with her brothers on the profit on a voyage to Vinland.) Some were local traders, who sold goods at the markets. Spinning and weaving, the quintessential feminine occupations, were often used to make money. Some houses had several rooms set aside where employees worked for the woman who owned the building, making cloth for sale. Women also were bakers, brewers, washers and cleaners. (In many cities during the Middle Ages, women were the main brewers, as well as making beer and fruit wines for the household.)

Women did the usual female things, midwifery, nursing and being servants. They also oversaw public morality, being hired by the government to catch servants who had gotten pregnant and tried to hide the fact. They could check female servants for breast milk, which was grounds for punishment if they were shown to be lactating.[83] (The punishment for being found with a baby or having milk in one's breasts was to be kicked out of town, so women were certainly going to conceal their pregnancy if they could.) Women also worked in the more unexpected field of building, both ships and houses.

Another job open to urban women was prostitution, which was surprisingly tolerated during the medieval period, although the Reformation condemned it. The medievals preferred the regulatory approach, and prostitutes were required to dress more simply than other women. To reinforce this, a law in Stockholm in 1459 ruled that they could not wear fur, silver or gold.[84] Around the same time in Denmark, women were required to wear red and black hoods, and live only in certain areas of towns (an early version of the red-light district). Earlier, the Vikings in Russia (around 750) had traded in prostitutes, but these women were slaves, who had little choice in the matter.

Wives

In Norse society, women seem to have been raised to be married. Women were raised to be obedient to the needs of the clan, which in those days was the basic family unit. They also had to avoid any stain on their honour as much as any Victorian woman; the double standard was well in place by the Viking age. While male sexual exploits were a proof of virility, women who were caught with a lover could be killed. The family arranged their marriages for them, and they might only know the groom-to-be slightly before the wedding.

Earlier German society also seems to have been very concerned with virginity, or at least the Roman writer Tacitus thought so: *Clandestine love-letters are unknown to men and women alike. Adultery is extremely rare, considering the size of the population...[t]hey have in fact no mercy on a wife who prostitutes her chastity.* He also comments that husbands paid a bride-price, instead of women bringing a dowry, and that the exchange of gifts was the main feature of the marriage ceremony.

In later Icelandic society, women were no more consulted about marriage than in first century Germany. They did not have any say in marriage negotiations, nor was it considered a good thing if they did. The laws in Iceland and Norway prior to Christianity state that the father or other male relations arranged the marriages of their female relatives.[85] Ironically, the right of a woman to consent to her marriage was introduced by the Christians, whose marriage laws required the consent of both parties. But while they managed to convince people in the noble classes to abide by this rule, the lower classes resisted the idea that women should choose their own marriage partners.[86]

The man made an offer to the woman's guardians, who then bargained for a good bride-price. If they reached agreement, they shook hands, which was the first of three ceremonies that made a marriage binding. The next was the actual ceremony, which took place within a year at most. Then "bride-ale" was drunk, and the groom led to the bride's bed by attendants with lights. The next morning he paid her compensation for her lost virginity.

If the couple later divorced, the woman kept her bride-price and the compensation money. Women could initiate divorce proceedings, too. In the sagas, out of twelve divorces, women demanded nine, and all of the five threats to divorce were issued by women. Grounds mentioned included: *...a slap, a family feud, incompatibility, an Icelandic variety of nonconsummation, a compromising wound, a fatal illness, the wearing of sexually inappropriate dress, and a mocking verse.*[87] (Inappropriate dress was the cause when Thorthr divorced Aud, who wore trousers. She continued to wear them.[88]) Either party could divorce by announcing the fact before witnesses, and no stigma seems to have attached to the divorced or remarried.

As well as wives, men could also have concubines. Harald Fairhair had nine wives, while Prince Haakon of Norway kept a "harem" of kidnapped women even when he was an old man.[89] All the sources indicate that men could keep concubines, who were generally either slaves or else captured foreign women. Wives apparently did not mind this arrangement, since the extra children, as property, contributed to the household. However, they often insisted that the other women not live in their household.

On the other hand, a woman could not have any other lovers. A man who seduced a married woman was punished by law. Kormakr was fined an ounce of gold per kiss after he kissed another man's wife.[90] To sleep with a woman was to be condemned to lesser outlawry. The woman's consent or lack thereof was not the issue; it seems that the Icelanders considered that the damage was to the woman's worth in marriage, or to her as some man's property. A rather ridiculous version was the ascending list of fines in Gotland for touching various parts of a woman's body.

Widows

Becoming a widow seems to have been a woman's surest route to power and influence. Many of the powerful queens were widows who exercised power in the name of their family, or as regents for their sons. Women grew in prestige as they aged, according to burial goods found in graves. The older the woman, the richer the goods, while men's graves became less well- endowed as they got older.[91] This was true for most of Scandinavia, and probably reflects both the values of a warrior society and the rarity of older women in an age when many died in childbirth or of diseases.

Once a woman became a widow, or came to maturity, she no longer had a male guardian, except in Iceland, where unmarried women always had to have a man to represent them. A woman whose husband was dead, or who was unmarried but had no near male relatives, could manage her own affairs or enter into business without inter- ference.

Nuns

After the Christian conversion, a new career opened up for women who did not wish to marry, or re-marry. Interestingly, women were not very quick to take it up, perhaps because of the lag between the official conversion and the actual dying-out of paganism.

By 1250 there were twenty-two nunneries in Denmark, and six in Sweden. Norway and Iceland, however, were more resistant to the idea, having only five in Norway and one in Iceland.[92] Some of them were endowed by women, and the nobles tended to be the inhabitants. Women also tended to be donors to churches and monasteries, to the point where some towers on Swedish churches were paid for by women. (Some of these towers also served as the tomb for the donor.) Poorer women often made donations to the convent in return for being looked after in their old age; they took less stringent vows and continued to live as laity.

The nunneries served primarily as a place for women who could not marry, or widows whose remarriage would have broken up family property. Some kings and nobles seem to have treated the nunneries as a sort of safety-deposit for marriageable relatives, putting them in and then taking them out to be married to advantage. Despite these rather cynical motives, however, there were women who entered nunneries willingly, and who wished to avoid marriage. In pre-modern times, wives tended to have a poor life expectancy, dying in childbirth or of hard work, so it is not surprising that women might want to avoid marrying.

Some heads of nunneries, being women of high birth and influence, were able to leave their print on history. Birgitta of Sweden was one of these, who managed to persuade King Magnus Eriksson to give her Vadstena for her community. From there she founded the Order of the Most Holy Trinity (the Brigantines), and made pronouncements on politics. For example, she condemned King Magnus for his expedition against the Latvians and Estonians, and tried to get the Pope to return to Rome. Her original convent was an intellectual centre of Europe during her time there.

Hildegard of Bingen was another strong leader, who began as prioress of the religious community at Jutta in Germany, then founded a convent at Rupertsberg and another at Eibingen. She was called the "Sibyl of the Rhine" for her visions, which made her famous even in her own day. She wrote books on many subjects, including medicine. These visions, along with her music, ensured her fame into the present day. Although she is not actually a saint, she receives veneration from Christians. Both Hildegard and Birgitta saw visions, and tried to influence politics with their insights, continuing the tradition of prophetic women who influenced events. Clearly retiring into a convent could give one influence, instead of removing one from the secular world.

Women in the Scandinavian world were able to use their power, even after Christianity arrived. There is a remarkable consistency in the accounts of Norse and German women, beginning with the Roman chroniclers and moving into the high Middle Ages. All agree that the women were strong, independent and relatively free.

Recommended Reading:

Women in the Viking Age, by Judith Jesch, Boydell, Woodbridge, Suffolk, Engl., 1991. This book covers women during the Viking Age both in life and in literature. It is well-argued and has many interesting things to say about the women and fictional heroines of the Norse.
Medieval Scandinavia by Birgit and Peter Sawyer, University of Minnesota, Minneapolis, 1993. This book has a very interesting chapter on women and their roles in Old Norse society.

Heroines

The heroines of the sagas and Eddic poems have contributed more to the idea of the strong, independent Norsewoman than any historian could do. However, this raises some important questions. Was their strength and independence admired, or were they simply male bogies the way the Amazons were for the Greeks? In this chapter, I will look at four of the famous Norse heroines, and try to determine what lessons can be learned from their stories.

Brynhild

In the popular mind, a Norse female would be some sort of warrior-maiden, an image influenced by the Valkyries. In literature, if not life, this image finds its truth. Shield-women like Brynhild were human women who were called Valkyries, and occupied a space between the human and the godlike. The story of Brynhild, in fact, is in many ways a story about boundaries between various categories.

Brynhild was one of Odin's valkyries, sworn to his service and to remain a virgin. Her full story appears in the *Volsung Saga*, which tells how she was a warrior until she disobeyed Odin's command and saved a man he had condemned to die. Odin pricked her with a "sleep-thorn" and doomed her to marriage. Sigurd later awoke her and they were betrothed. She then took up maidenly pursuits at her father's castle, and Sigurd met her again there and renewed their vows. From there he goes to Gjuki's court, where he drank a potion of forgetfulness, and married Gjuki's daughter Gudrun.

Next Gunnarr, Gudrun's brother, decided he wanted to marry Brynhild, and he and Sigurd set off to woo her. Sigurd overcame the wall of fire around her castle, and courted her disguised as Gunnarr. She married Gunnarr, because she had vowed to marry only a man heroic enough to cross a wall of fire. Despite this, their three nights together are spent with a sword between them in the bed (because he was not her real husband). Brynhild was already pregnant by Sigurd from their previous meeting, but they celebrated the wedding at Gjuki's court. Gudrun and Brynhild quarrelled, and Gudrun told her that Sigurd fooled her into marrying Gunnarr.

After this, all three parties tried to restore peace with Brynhild, but she demanded only that Gunnarr kill Sigurd and his sons, to wipe out the stain on their marriage. When Gunnarr got a relative to kill Sigurd, Brynhild acted like she was pleased, but inside she was sorrowful, for she only loved Sigurd. Now she told Gunnarr about the sword between them when Sigurd wooed her in Gunnarr's form, and reproached him for killing his sworn brother. She distributed her gold and stabbed herself with a sword, after she had Gunnarr build a pyre for her and Sigurd.

This ending is by no means the only one, although it is the most widely known. In some versions of her story, she survived to enjoy the vengeance she had taken. As Andersson thinks, she can be seen in these versions as a tragic heroine like many men in the Norse sagas, who have to kill near relatives or break important oaths to reach their goals.[93] The conventional ending reflects the growing medieval interest in romantic love, which in this version brings down the maiden warrior. Depending on which way one looks at it, either she avenged the deception which made her break her oath, or else she dies of sorrow after killing her true love.

The tension between these two version of the events lead to another aspect of the story: her warrior-maiden status and later more "feminine" behaviour. Until the sleep-thorn, she behaves like an independent female. After that, she went back to her father's control, and prepared for the fate Odin has "cursed" her with: marriage. Notice that she took up embroidery and weaving, waiting patiently for her man. The oath about only marrying the most heroic man around, however, was more in keeping with her former role. She married Gunnarr, who suffered through the rest of the story for his lack of heroism. Her former status as warrior came back to haunt him, as his wife was more heroic than him, as was the man she thought she had married.

Since Brynhild was no longer a warrior, she had to seek revenge through her husband. It seems that as soon as she had sex, she lost her ability as a warrior. She still managed a heroic end, dying in the prescribed manner for those who wished to live in Valhalla. (If one died off the battle-field, being stabbed with a spear or sword ensured that Odin took you.) She constantly switched back and forth between the feminine and masculine modes as the ancient Norse defined them, a polarity expressed as the weaving woman versus the warrior man.

Gudrun

Gudrun did not come off well in Brynhild's story, and indeed throughout all the sagas and Eddic poems she appeared in, she was a woman one wouldn't want to cross. In her defence, she was provoked to insult Brynhild because Brynhild insulted her husband.

After Sigurd's death, she married King Atli, who is often considered to be the same person as the historical Attila, although obviously his character has been changed somewhat. Atli began to want the hoard of gold that Sigurd had owned, and laid a trap for Gudrun's brothers so that he could learn from them where it was. Gudrun sent them a message warning them of her husband's plan, but to no avail. When they arrived, Atli tortured them, but they died without telling him where the gold was. To avenge her brothers, Gudrun killed her two sons by Atli, and served them to him for dinner, then told him what she had done. Later that night she stabbed him in his bed, set fire to his hall, and escaped.

Later her daughter Svanhita was married to a king Jormunrek. He had her trampled by horses after some of his courtiers deceived him into thinking that she had been unfaithful to him. When Gudrun heard of this, she demanded that her two sons (by her third husband) go and kill Jormunrek in retaliation. At first they were reluctant, but her taunts stung them into action. When they told her they would go, she laughed with joy and gave them armour. Unfortunately, they did not heed her advice and so were killed by Jormunrek.

Gudrun's history seems to delineate two forms of female revenge. On the one hand, a woman could step outside the female role and take vengeance herself, as Gudrun and Brynhild did. Or, as they both did, she could incite her male relatives to take revenge for her. This reflects a historical reality: since women were unable to appear at the things to bring charges or act as witnesses, they either had to get a man to do it for them, or else try for private revenge. Women often incite men to violence in the sagas because there was no reason for them to seek justice and compensation.

Gudrun's story, even more than Brynhild's, is that of a person who takes righteous revenge after insufferable wrongs. It takes on an element of Medea-like tragedy, since she not only kills Atli but wipes out his patrimony by killing his sons. In patriarchal societies that is a shrewd blow for a woman, even if it does mean killing one's own children. The difference is that while the Greeks treated Medea as a sort of monster, Gudrun's deed is more an assertion of family loyalty against one who broke faith with her and her family. This element was perhaps what made the difference for the clan-oriented Norse. Unlike Medea, Gudrun didn't weep or express remorse. She was more like a female Charles Bronson, who sought revenge and was satisfied by it.

Sigrun

By contrast, Sigrun came down on the side of the man who slew her father and brother. Her story is in the *Poetic Edda* in two versions; there are significant differences between them. In the first, she was a Valkyrie who appeared to Sigurd's half-brother Helgi and told him that he must kill the man she was supposed to marry, and tells him off for trying to seduce her. After Helgi agreed to defeat her suitor, she followed him into the battle and protected him. Afterward, she announced his victory, and promised him both marriage and riches.

The second version, in *Helgaqvitha Hundingsbana onnor*, showed a much more lovelorn version of Sigrun, who was less independent of Helgi. She met him once and challenged him, but when she saw him again in her father's hall, she fell in love and suddenly instead of a

Valkyrie who flies through the air and knows Helgi's deeds through her powers, she transformed into a maiden who told Helgi that she could not marry him because her father would be angry. Judith Jesch calls his reply to this "patronising":

> *"Pay no heed to Hogni's wrath,*
> *or to your kinsmen's cruel hearts!*
> *From now on, maiden, you shall be mine,*
> *and none of your family do I fear."*

And she is right.

During the battle with Sigrun's suitor, Helgi killed her father and brother, who were on his side. Sigrun married him anyway, and they had several sons. But, her kinsman Dag adhered to the vengeance code, and killed Helgi. He then rode to Sigrun and told her what he had done, and when she swore to avenge Helgi, he reproached her for continuing strife among the family, and gave her compensation. She visited Helgi's ghost in its barrow, affirming her love for him. Later, she died of grief.

The variations in Sigrun's story were caused in part by the fact that a new ideology of romantic love was coming to replace the older dramas of kinship and revenge. But notice how much of Sigrun's power is lost in the second version.

Although Helgi said that she had been his shield-maiden, the text said nothing about her protecting him during the battle. Her identity as a Valkyrie serves only to make him a greater hero; as soon as he came on the scene, she became another princess to be rescued.

While it was still part of the hero's image to have a Valkyrie or fylgia to protect one, Sigrun's actual role was reduced to nil. The romantic function that Sigrun played in the second version makes her a lesser character than in the first one.

Bergthora

In *Njals Saga*, Bergthora was the ideal wife. She even chose to die with her husband Njal when he was burnt in his house. During her life she was a húsfreyar, managing a large farm. When a man came looking for work, she told him, "*I am Njal's wife...and I have as much say in hiring servants as he*"[94] She also played a part in his death, although not wittingly. When she gets into a feud with her neighbour Hallgerdr (another housewife of similar status) Hallgerdr had a skald satirise Bergthora's husband and sons, so she incited them to kill Hallgerdr's husband. Neither the writer or her family seemed to blame her for this, even though it ended in tragedy.

Both the women were described as proud and stiff, made of the same sort of stuff as Gudrun. However, Bergthora definitely came off better than Hallgerdr, which was probably because of her loyalty to her husband. Hallgerdr was much more stubborn, and she quarrelled with her husband several times throughout the saga.

In answer to the questions raised in the beginning of this chapter, it seems that women who took vengeance, or who incited their menfolk to do so, were not necessarily seen as evil or troublemakers. In life this may have been different, but in sagas family honour and revenge are the main motors of the plot. Strong women who could avenge slights, or encourage men to avenge them, were necessary to the stories. It may have also had some resonance in life, where women had no voice in the compensation process and so no reason to pursue it. As for women who acted as warriors, the sagas do not condemn them the way that the Greeks did the Amazons. Nor do the stories of Gudrun and Brynhild call them unnatural, just heroic, as their men were heroic.

Mysteries

This chapter considers pagan religion from the point of view of women's worship. While much is written about the cults of Odin, Thor and Freyr, there is not so much on household cults, or worship of the goddesses. The sources, written during the incursion of a religion with a central male deity, are less than forthcoming about these parts of Norse religion. I have tried to pull together what I could find, from the Eddic poems, sagas and later folklore.

Women's Patrons

In Snorri Sturluson's *Edda*, he tells us that maidens go to Gefjon after they die. Despite her own ambiguous status, Gefjon was clearly a patron of young unmarried women, rather like the Greek Kore/Persephone. Presumably women also swore by Gefjon, as the maiden did in the *Volsa thattr*. Freya also took women after death; in one saga a woman killed herself after her warrior lover died, she told her family she wouldn't eat again until she was in Freya's hall. Since Freya got first pick of warriors, it seems likely that women who went to Freya had died a valiant death. (Which may explain why women killed themselves when their husbands or lovers died - they wanted to die heroically as well.) Frigg was the goddess of married women, just as Hera was for Greek matrons.

Women called on Freya and Frigg to make them fertile, especially Frigg. In the *Oddrúnargrátr*, the handmaid called on the two goddesses to bless the midwife. In *Sigrdrífumál*, Sigrdrifa tells Sigurth:

Learn help runes eke,   if help thou wilt
a woman to bring forth her babe:
  on thy palms wear them
and grasp her wrists,   and ask the disir's aid.

These goddesses, who may have overlapped with Frigg and Freya, were involved in women's matters generally. That they should have presided at birth is not surprising.

Birth rites

The earliest references to midwives was the Old High German word hevianna, from *hafjan(d)jō, "the lifting one", and anna, "woman" (another derivation gives ana, "grandmother, ancestor".).[95] This would certainly seem to fit the job of midwife. The custom was for a woman in labour to kneel or squat on cowhide, or carpet strewn with herbs. Then someone would paint runes on her hands, and after the birth the baby was laid on the ground so it could absorb strength from the earth.[96]

Another birth-spell was an Anglo-Saxon charm that used both pagan and Christian elements. It mentioned Mary and Elizabeth because they both bore famous sons, and the second part of the charm told the story of Lazarus, and used the words "Lazarus come forth". Then new sticky wax was put under the woman's right foot, to draw the child out. The earlier versions of the charm mention Freya, the later ones the Virgin Mary.[97]

In *Oddrúnargrátr*, Oddrun came to the aid of the servant Borgny, who was unable to give birth. Oddrun came into the house, and:

> *Then they talked   no more together;*
> *Oddrun went to Borgny   and brought her help,*
> *chanting strong spells   and magic charms,*
> *mighty witchcraft   for the woman's need.*
> (Terry)

While the poem doesn't tell what she chanted, it may have been an invocation to either the disir or the Norns, both of whom were involved with births.

The Norns were offered a meal of porridge after the child was born, and this was called "Norns' groats": nornegrøten in Setesdal, nauegrot in Telemark, Norway and nornegreytu in the Faroe Islands.[98]

In the Faroe Islands the mother had this for her first meal after the labour, presumably in the Norns' stead. The Norns also put marks on the child's nails, with white ones being especially lucky.[99] This may come from a verse in the *Sigrdrífmál* about where the first runes were cut:

> *the nail of a Norn,   a night-owl's beak*
> (Terry)

Several spells and verses in the sagas mention cutting runes in one's nails for magical effects.

In the Fafnismál the Norns are also mentioned as attending at births:

> *Sigurd said:*
> *"Tell me, Fafnir,   famed for your wisdom-*
> * I know you've learned much lore,*
> *what Norns will help   women in their need*
> * before they give birth?"*

135

Fafnir said:

> *"The Norns descend   from different races,*
> *they have no common kin,*
> *some from the gods, some from the elves,*
> *some are Dvalin's daughters."*
> (Terry)

The answer would seem to be that each race had to look to their own norns for help.

The Dísír

The Dísir, or "Goddesses" were generally patrons of women, and had their own festival during the fall. In the times when the Christians were missionizing, one group of women were burnt alive in a house rather than give up celebrating the Dísir's feast. In *Heidrek's Saga*, a woman reddens the altar with blood, late at night.[100] The festival was also an occasion for heavy drinking. In *Viga-Glum's Saga*, the friends and relations of a householder gather in his home and celebrate the feast together. It seems that these deities were reverenced by both men and women.

This event often took place in a private home, but there were also disarsalr, "halls of the dísir", where people made sacrifices to the goddesses. The *Heimskringla* says that there was a Disirblot at Uppsala, the large public temple in Sweden. King Aldis was there, and when he rode his horse through the temple the horse stumbled, and he fell off and died. There was also a court held at this time, called the Disathing, and a market.[101]

The Dísir were usually connected to a particular family, perhaps as deified ancestors. Many of the household temples, which would have served for family worship,

136

were probably dedicated to them.[102] As part of the family they had an unchancy aspect; in both *Reginsmal* and the *Greenlandish Lay of Atli,* they abandon the men and thus cause them to die. In *Reginsmal,* "*Will guileful disir on either side of thee would fain see thee fall*". (Hollander) In the *Greenlandish Lay of Atli,* Glaumvor has a dream that her husband will die if he goes into battle:

Methought in the darkness	*came dead women hitherward,*
clad in weeds of mourning,	*and wished to fetch thee,*
beckoned and bade thee	*to their benches forthwith:*
I fear that the goddesses	*have given thee over.*

(Hollander)

In both cases, the men are doomed as soon as the disir desert them. Another story says how a man dreamt that women in white and women in black were battling for his soul; in this case Christian influence has caused the Disir to be split into good and bad.

The Disir could also be protective, in a role similar to that of the fylgur. In *Thorstien Vikinsson,* the main character told another man, "Now we must separate for some time, and fare thee well. I tell thee that my Disir will constantly follow thee."[103] Apparently a man could send his Disir with someone, just as the fylgia (a protective spirit) could be transferred among family members.

Freya and Skadhi were both called dis: Vanadis or "Lady of the Vanir", and Öndurdis "Snowshoe Lady". While it could also mean any goddess, and it tended to be used as a plural for all the goddesses, some writers assume that Freya and Skadhi had a special relation to the Disir. All three of them were associated with danger or death: Freya

137

as a war-goddess, Skadhi both by name and her warrior-aspect, and the Disir by foretelling death and disaster. The Disir had their festival during "Winternights" and Skadhi was the goddess of winter. Freya may have been the major female ancestor in her role as keeper of the dead, just as Freyr was associated with the dead in mounds. This would link her with the female ancestral spirits, the Disir.

The Norse don't seem to have made sharp distinctions between the Disir and the other categories of women spirits, either. The Norns and the Valkyries are called Disir in some places, and their functions tend to overlap. The goddesses and the ancestral females may have shared worship at the disablot, since both were Disir.

A women's ritual

In *St. Olaf's Saga*, the main character takes refuge in an isolated farm during the darkest part of the year. During his visit, a dead horse's penis is brought to the house, and the housewife treats it reverently, preserving it with herbs and wrapping it. That evening it was passed from hand to hand, every person in the house reciting some verses as they handled it. It was offered up to the mörnir, in the following way:

May the mörnir accept this gift.

Then, some women came forward:

Bring the staff
To the bride-women
they shall the rod moisten in the evening.

Unfortunately, then the saint threw the völsi (penis) into the fire, so the rest of the ritual remains unknown.

What is the meaning of this ritual? The sexual aspect seems obvious, since "bride-women" were given a penis to "moisten". (Folke Ström thinks that this ritual was to ensure the fertility of horses.[104]) The time of year is winter, before Yule, which leads us to the goddess of winter, Skadhi. She was called Mörn in the poem *Haustlöng*, and the mörnir ("ogresses") are a sub-group of the giantesses. Since Skadhi is both a goddess of the cold wastes, and a sexual goddess who had liaisons with Loki, Odin and Njord, this ritual seems to pertain to her. An odd sidelight on this ritual occurs in a story about Gefjon, discussed earlier in this book. In it, a woman calls on Gefjon to witness that she is forced to "take" a penis. This could mean that she was being made to participate in this ritual.

Women's Goddesses

Although most of this book is about Norse goddesses, this section is going to have a more Germanic focus. Beings like Perchta and Holda, both West-Germanic deities, probably carried on the traditions of women's religion, which were not recorded in the sources. I think that some of their attributes can be connected to the Norse goddesses, in ways which will illuminate the rather scanty material we have on them.

These Germanic figures are very often the prototype of the housewifely goddess, who spins, raises good children, and keeps an eye on the stores. This would suggest that they are descendants of Frigg, and Davidson seems to think this as well.[105] Some of these also have more witchy aspects, and this I would relate to Freya. Goddesses in this category also tend to be more sexual, which would fit with the Norse love-goddess. (Notice also how this replicated the good-bad split in sexist images of women.)

These goddesses, whose names vary throughout Germany, generally have a holiday, usually in the Christmas season, but not one of the important Christian dates. I infer two things from this. First, that these goddesses were accommodated to, and perhaps are no older than, Christian tradition in Germany. Second, that the holiday picked for these is the older holiday of Mother-night. Bede mentions this in his calendar, and it would be an appropriate festival for these particular figures to take over, as the festival's name seems to indicate that it was in honour of female ancestors.

Along with this festival, there were certain rules that any woman who wanted the favour of the goddess had to obey. (Some of these were probably also useful for enforcing social norms, such as working hard, raising quiet children, etc.) There seem to be many taboos concerning spinning, which was one of the commonest of women's chores. When you consider that every piece of clothing, every towel, and all the linen was spun and woven, you begin to understand the centrality of spinning to women's lives. Two of the goddesses, one from Silesia and one Switzerland, are called Spillalutsche and Frau Chunkle, from words for spindle and distaff, respectively.

Although women must have felt that they were born spinning and would die spinning, there were times when spinning was ritually forbidden. In most places the spinning had to be finished before Christmastime, or (depending on the region) Percht, Frau Chunkle or Frau Holle would either tangle, lose or dirty your distaff. In some areas any spinning during this time was severely punished by the goddesses. In Zwettel the Spinnweibel would come and twist the flax of anyone spinning during Christmas. In northern Germany, neither windlasses nor spinning wheels could turn from Christmas until New Year's Day.[106]

In Thüringa, near the Hörselberg, girls would put fibre on their distaffs on Christmas Eve, and try to finish it by Epiphany. Frau Holle also starts her rounds on Dec. 24, and so the girls try to clear their distaffs before she returns. When she starts, the girls have a rhyme: "so many hairs, so many good years". On her return, however, "so many hairs, so many bad years".[107]

The goddesses' attitude towards the housewife is ambivalent. On the one hand, they are willing to help those with too much to do, like Frau Holle, who helped women carry their loads. She was known to spin a reel full overnight, for industrious types.[108] But, if the woman didn't seem to be putting in honest effort, she would find that her house was in a worse state than ever after Perchta or Frau Holle or whoever had passed. In an early version of social work, the goddess would take the children if a house in the lower Styria wasn't clean enough.[109] They often punished or took children who were naughty as well. Sometimes this involved heavy labour to improve the children's behaviour, which suggests that the Tories had a hand in it.

Sometimes, although not very often, the goddesses gave children. A community near Caldonazzo in the Italian Tyrol believed that to get children a woman had to visit the goddess in her cave, where she kept unborn children in water barrels. Another way to get pregnant was to bathe in a pond called the Frauhollenteich, near the Meissner.[110] Sometimes the goddesses appeared in the sky, along with a troop of children, but these were usually unbaptised souls, rather than potential humans.

These goddesses have many similarities to Frigg, although the Norse sources don't really give enough information for a proper comparison. There are, however, some similarities between them. According to MacCulloch,

> *In Sweden, at the religious observance of Thursday, when the house was prepared for the visit of deities, the expression was used 'Hallow the god Thor and Frigg.' On the same day no spindle or distaff could be used, for Frigg herself then span. In the evening an old man and woman might be seen sitting at the distaff, viz., Thor and Frigg.*[111]

Orion's Belt was called Frigg's Distaff by the Germans. She gave a child to King Rerir in the *Volsung Saga*, by having her attendant Gna drop an apple in his lap.

Other aspects of these goddesses were less domestic. They were frequently associated with the Wild Hunt, a riot of spirits that rode the night winds. Even St. Lucy was sometimes said to lead a parade of trolls and other monsters during Christmas season. Another version of the wild chase was the troop of women who rode to the "*wake of Perchta*"[112]. In some parts of Germany, the witches' ride was called Holle-riding, and the wild hunt led naturally into the idea of the witches' sabbat. A Church Canon condemns women who said they had ridden with a crowd of demons, with the "witch Holda" as their leader.[113]

A goddess who was intimately associated with the Wild Hunt was Herodias, a very witchy female. The Christian legend had it that she was condemned to wander with demons because as Herod's daughter she had enticed him to behead John the Baptist. She was one of a group, along with Holda, Diana, and Perchta, who led the witches' ride. The witches rode to their nocturnal sabbats, with one of these goddesses at the head. This could be connected, in a very tenuous way, to the Valkyrie ride, perhaps led by Freya. Another connection is the way that these goddesses are all associated with the dead. Freya took the slain to her hall, while these goddesses accept the souls of dead children, and sometimes lead trains of spirits across the sky.

Both the medieval ideas of the witch, striga and maleficia, could have applied to Freya. The striga was the lascivious version of the witch, who was accused of provoking lust and copulating with demons. Maleficia were those who caused harm to others by magic. Freya was the sex-goddess of the north, who had slept with all the Æsir and elves. As a strife-stirring goddess, she had a great deal of potential to cause harm. The seithr she supposedly taught Odin had harmful applications, and most of the accounts of its use focus on the harm it could do. (See the chapter on seithr for more on this.)

Runes

Thence wise maidens   *three betake them-*
under spreading boughs *their bower stands-*
[Urth one is hight,   *the other Verthandi,*
Skuld the third: *they scores did cut,*
(Hollander)

In this part of the book, we are going to look at the runes and their meanings. The runes themselves are, at their most basic, an alphabet to write with. Each rune represents one sound. Like the alphabet, which is named for its first two letters, the runes are also called the Futhark, after the first six letters ("th" is one rune). Their angular shapes are the result of being designed for carving rather than writing. Runes were cut into stone, wood, and metal, either to convey a message or for magical purposes. Later, when people began to use paper for writing, the runic shapes grew more cursive.

The runes are also a symbol-system. Each rune has a name which is also a word. The rune-poems of the Anglo-Saxons and Scandinavians give these names along with the rune's meaning, although to the new reader these poems can seem impossibly cryptic. However, these give insight into the culture and beliefs of the Germanic peoples, although from a mostly male point of view.

Recently, some authors have tried to develop meanings for the runes that illuminate women's experiences. These rely on reinterpretation of the meanings of the rune-names and shapes to give new insights into women's use of the runes (see the list at the end of the chapter). This section will give my interpretations of the runes, based on female experience and goddesses.

The idea of women's runes brings up the question of women's use of the runic systems. These were the property of the intelligentsia, since most people were illiterate. In some of the sagas women carve runes, either for spells or mundane use, so it's not obvious that a woman couldn't use them. There were also women skalds (poets) who were versed in the lore of the runes and of the myths and legends of their people. A piece of a loom found in Germany was incised, "Blithgund wrote these runes". This was a standard formula for runemasters and runemistresses. In *Sigrdrifumal*, the Valkyrie Sigrdrifa instructs the hero in the use of runes for victory and other matters. In the *Song of Atli* Gudrun sends a runic message to Kostbera, who sees that the messenger has changed the runes.[114]

Runic meanings

This listing concentrates on their meanings from a feminist perspective. I touch on some of the conventional meanings as well, and at the end of the chapter I list some books that cover the normal runes in more detail.

The runic system I will describe here is the Elder Futhark, which has 24 letters. These are further divided into three groups of eight runes each. Some writers assign significance to this arrangement of aetts (families, eights) and name them after the first letter of each: Freya's Aett, Heimdall's Aett, and Tyr's Aett.

Freya's Aett naturally deals with prosperity, fertility, and the powers of the Vanir. Heimdall's Aett seems to incorporated a seasonal myth, since it begins with hail and ends with sun, the harvest rune balancing the two. Tyr's Aett is oriented towards humanity and Midgard.

Freya's Aett

Feoh (cattle): Since cattle were the main form of wealth in early societies, the meaning of this rune is wealth or prosperity. This relates to the energising potential of Feoh. In feminine terms this rune clearly relates to Freya as the giver of wealth, who wept gold and amber. Poets referred to gold as Freya's tears. Her two daughters were named "Treasure", and her status as one of the Vanir means that she was also part of the wealth of fertility in land and animals.

Ur (aurochs): The aurochs was a large animal rather like a musk ox, which is now extinct. They were powerful animals, and so Ur is about primal power and strength. This is usually interpreted as virility, but men don't have any monopoly on strength and power. Its female equivalent is Audhumbla, who was the first animal. Using the ice as a salt-lick, she freed the primal ancestor, Buri. She also nourished the giant Ymir, whose body was broken up to make the world. (In one legend a Valkyrie appears as an aurochs.)

THorn (giant): Giants were the enemies of the gods, but at the same time some of them were their parents or lovers. Nanna and Gerd were both giantesses, who married Baldr and Freyr. This rune relates to the might of the giants, but also to the might of Thor. The female counterpart is Thrud ("power"). It represents defence in the passive sense, just like thorns. The Old Icelandic Rune-Poem says that Thorn is "*the sickness of women*" and the Old Norwegian Rune-Poem calls it "*the torment of women*"[115], which is probably the monthly "illness" of menstruation. Thorn was also the rune that Skirnir carved to curse Gerd with frenzy, filth and lust when she refused to marry Freyr.

As (god/mouth): This rune relates to speech, reason and the conscious mind. It also relates to the word for god, Ase. Because of its links to speech and the mind, it is usually related to Odin. The feminine of Ase is Asynia, and this rune relates to the sky-goddesses as well as the gods. The foremost sky-goddess is Frigg, so she can be assigned to this rune. Unlike Odin, Frigg does not express her wisdom in speech, although in the myth of Baldr's death she acts on her insights. All acts of communication or magical incantation fall under this rune. This includes galdr and probably seithr, the women's magic, as well.

Raido (chariot): The usual meaning of this rune is travel or movement. One interpretation of this rune is the chariot of the sun-goddess Sól or Sunna, who rides through the sky each day. It relates to all cyclical movement, such as the round of the seasons. Both the sun and moon measure time by their travels, ordering life into days, months and years. A model of a horse and chariot carrying a sun-wheel from the Bronze Age suggests that people knew of this ordering early on, and respected its power over their lives.

Ken (torch): The light of the house and feasting-hall is the significance of this rune. Ken also relates to the hearth-fire, a specifically female domain. Humans made and maintained both, by learning to control fire. This understanding relates to the verb "to ken", which is also part of this rune's meaning. Ancient peoples often saw the fire in the hearth as a goddess whom they gave offerings at mealtimes and special occasions. Hearth-fires and torches were the only light in olden times, so the rune also symbolises light, and perhaps consciousness, by analogy. The fire also relates to female sexual fire, by a pun with the rune name.

Gyfu (gift): This rune relates to sacrifice, which ensures the bond between the deities and us, and gifts given among humans, which bind the community together. In Germanic culture it was important to be seen as generous, especially for nobles who had to keep their followers' loyalty. Marriage also comes under Gyfu, as both partners give themselves. The custom of giving a woman in marriage to cement an alliance is another kind of gift-exchange. (The rune later became the sign for a kiss, so it is closely connected with love and marriage.) Gefjon rules this rune, since it is a rune of giving.

Wynn (joy): When things do go right, humans rejoice along with their deities. Happiness is something we all strive for. When we achieve our goals we naturally celebrate with our families and friends. It isn't surprising that joy comes at the end of the first aett, since it encourages us to set time aside to celebrate what we have done so far, before we continue into the next task. Pennick suggests that the rune represents a flag or banner. When men went to war, women embroidered their flags to bring them luck in battle.[116] In several sagas the women's banners brought victory to the side that carried them.

Heimðall's Aett

Hagel (hail): Hail is a destructive force, as anyone who has ever watched it level crops will know. The devastation it can wreak is hard on farmers, watching their year's work being killed. The storm is a dramatic change from the peace of Wynn, and seems like a disruption. However, transformation is part of our lives, even if it seems as violent as a storm. The lesson of Hagel is to expect change and work with it, and of course to prepare for disaster.

Nyd (need): One of the unpleasant realities of life is need in its various forms. The difference in want and need is something we all should learn, but for our ancestors it was a far starker contrast. This rune relates to Gyfu, the giving rune, since need has to be succoured. The Norns rule this rune, since they send fortunes. The binding that they cause by weaving the web of wyrd is one of the meanings of this rune. The Anglo-Saxon rune-poem says that while need is painful, it is a blessing to those who heed it in time.

Is (ice): This is a winter rune, and a cosmic one, since ice and fire formed the worlds in Norse myth. The Germanic people thought of the two elements as opposites. Ice is a freezing that prevents motion or change, and covers the land with barrenness. Ice covered the Germanic lands for much of the year, and the people appreciated its beauty while fearing its power. This is the rune of Skadhi, the winter goddess. (Some writers associate Hagel, Nyd and Is with the three Norns.)

Jera (year, harvest): The harvest is the theme of this rune, with its intimations of completion and abundance. Harvest implies that the work has been done, and now the worker reaps the results. As the culmination of the year, the rune points to the balancing of the forces of the year. The shape of the rune reflects this. (Dag, the final rune, also has a dual shape, this time joined-up to show completion.) The shape also resembles a double spiral. This could represent movement into the centre and out again, which would correspond with both completion and the cycle of the year. The turning motion it implies fits well with Jera's link to Yule, and the beginning of the sun's revival. This rune also relates to Fulla as the goddess of the harvest.

Eoh (yew/sedge): The great tree Yggdrasil that held the nine worlds together was either of yew or ash, so this rune has cosmic significance. It also relates to shamanism, since its practitioners travelled to the worlds by moving up and down the tree. Bows were made of yew, so the rune also conveys the idea of resilience, since the wood should bend but not break. Aswynn suggests it means venturing forth, like the arrow fired off. This rune also relates to Skadhi, the winter goddess who hunted with her yew-bow.

Peorth (dice-cup): A dice-cup is a powerful symbol of the wyrd that shapes human lives, as well as the womb that we all come from. The interaction of chance and destiny, along with the interventions of humans, fascinated the Germans. This rune is associated with the Norns, shapers of destinies. As well as the great Norns, there were three that appeared at births, and set the child's fortune. Two of these gave gifts like generosity or courage, while the third always gave a shortcoming, like an evil tongue or stinginess.

Elhaz (elk/moose): This animal is the European elk, which North Americans call the moose. The rune is a stylised representation of the tines of its horns. Another suggestion is that it represents a splayed hand, which corresponds with its association with defence. It can also represent the swan, in which case the rune is its footprint. In this form Elhaz is the rune of the Valkyries, who were swan-maidens as well as warriors. The Anglo-Saxon Rune Poem calls it elk-sedge, which cut the hand that tried to grasp it. All the meanings can be related to an alternative translation of the rune-name: "protection".

Sigel (sun): The sun-goddess is the force behind this rune. She destroys ice and frost and brings the gentle warmth of summer. This rune brings victory in all struggles, just as the sun triumphs over darkness, and even the end of the world. (Her daughter will ride in the sky in the world that appears after the destruction of the present one.) The sun in Northern myth destroyed ice-giants and dwarves with her rays, and nurtured with her gentle heat.

Tyr's Aett

Tyr (pole-star): This rune' s form is that of a spindle, which is connected to women's work and magic. Frigg was the chief sky-goddess, so we can associate her with this rune, and the constellation Frigg's Distaff (Orion's Belt) shows her connection with spinning.

Frigg wove the clouds and made the rain, and later superstition said that on Thursday no woman could spin, because Frigg was doing her work. Spinning and weaving were an important part of women's mysteries in those days. Since the stars of the Zodiac were thought to turn around Frigg's Distaff, she too is an upholder of law. (Tyr was the god of lawmaking and justice.)

Berkana (birch): The birch tree was important to the Germanic peoples, since it is one of the few deciduous trees that grows in the far north. In springtime children go out early, and bring home birch branches to strike their elders with. This custom is known as birching, and renews vitality. It drove out the evils of winter so that the good of spring and summer could move in. While many see Berkana as a birth-rune, the birch seems to represent purification more than birth. It can represent renewal, since anyone who lives in northern areas knows that it is the only deciduous tree there, and so when its buds appear spring is on the way.

Ehwaz (horse): The horse was a sacred animal to the Germans, as to all the Indo-Europeans. With it people could travel more quickly than on foot, which gave horses the sort of status cars have today. The Alcis were twin horse-gods worshipped by the Germanii. Some speculate that they fit into an Indo-European pattern of twins who rescue the sun-maiden every spring, thus returning fertility to the land. They did this by racing through a maze, which brings us back to the speed of the horse. They may also have drawn the sun's chariot through the sky.[117]

Mannaz (human): This rune means human being, not just "man". The original human beings were Ask and Embla, whom the gods made from an ash and an elm. Ask was the first man, and Embla the first woman. It is interesting that these two were a combination of natural material (wood) and the attributes that Odin and his brothers gave them (form, intelligence, soul). This rune is also related to the moon-god, Mani, who harmonises intuition and linear thinking.[118]

Lagu (water): Water to the Germans was both life and death. They were sea-faring people, who depended on water for transportation. However, there are evil spirits in the water, and the goddess Ran who wrecks ships. However, on the plus side there was the Frisian goddess Nehellenia who protected seafarers and gave fecundity. Water and fertility often go together, especially in the land of the Vanir. The ebb and flow of tides are also part of Lagu, a rune of cycles. Another meaning for Lagu is "leek", which sprang up in the sun's footsteps.[119] The sun's return began a new cycle and brought fertility, and the leek was a fertility-symbol as well.

Ing (the god Ing): the diamond-shaped version is a female one, according to Nigel Pennick.[120] The diamond shape is reminiscent of a vulva, which accords with the fertility aspect of Freyr. As an enclosed shape, it could represent the enclosed womb, with the child growing to fullness inside, or else the seed before it sprouts. The rune is connected to ancestry and the Disir (clan spirits). Each new birth adds to the clan, and the Disir hold the wisdom of the ancestors in keeping for the new life. The female counterpart of Ing is Nerthus, who also travelled in a wagon, while Pennick further associates the rune with a Danish goddess, Yngona.

Odal (ancestral land): This rune relates to the goddesses of Earth, especially Erda and Jörd. On a more mundane level, it represents the homestead, which was where women worked. As the inheritance, it refers both to the genetic material passed on by the parents and the kin-fyglia, a feminine spirit who embodied the luck and might of the family. In the Northern tradition reincarnation operates through the family line. In ancient times people often handed on their attributes to relatives just before they died. Another set of goddesses, the Disir, are also part of this rune's meanings. They represented the deified female ancestors, who looked out for their descendants' interests. Since ancestors were tied to (and sometimes buried on) the homestead, the family and its land were intimately connected.

Dag (day): This rune is precisely opposite to Jera, which is the rune of harvest and autumn. Dag stands for spring and dawn, and so it is the rune of the spring goddess Oestre, whose name also is associated with east and thus dawn. The rune indicates a turning point, the poise where opposites balance. This rune relates to Syn, the goddess of the door, who kept out harmful influences and attracted good ones. The position of Dag at the end of the

153

runic cycle makes it the rune of completion and highlights its meaning as the bringer of light, associated with hope and the ending of darkness.

Divination

In Tacitus' *Germanica*, he describes how the Germans would perform divination with twigs cut from a fruit-bearing tree. The *Völuspá* also mentions that the deities used runes:

The Æsir meet   *in Idavöll;*
they speak together   *about the Serpent,*
consider all   *that came to pass,*
the ancient runes   *offered to Odin.*
(Hollander)

This could mean either the runes as Odin originally learned them, or else his knowledge of what the future held, which led him to prepare for Ragnarök. At any rate, the use of runes for divination was well-established among the Germanic peoples.

Since the runes are generally thought of as tools for prediction rather than magic or writing, this section will cover how to use the runes for that purpose. Some people like to make a ceremony of divination. They might want to get a white or blue cloth to cast their runes on, and either just throw them onto the cloth and read them like that, or use one of the layouts below. An invocation to the Norns and Odin would go well with rune-casting.

Making your own runes is an important part of magical rune-casting. According to Tacitus the runes were cut from fruit or nut bearing trees each time a cast was made, but one can just make a permanent set to use.

154

Ideally you should cut your runes into slips of wood, then redden the marks in the wood with blood or ochre. If this isn't possible you could make them from clay, either inlaying some red clay for the runes or painting them on. At the very least, mark them with a red pen on white cardboard (file cards are good). That way it will have a little bit of your energy in it, which pre-made runes that you buy won't. As you make each rune, hum the letter it symbolises to yourself. This "tunes it in" to the magical frequency it represents.

A note on buying runes: if you can't be bothered to make them, buying runes is a perfectly acceptable way to get a set. However, you will note that many include a blank rune, called Wyrd, which I did not mention above. This rune, which represents fate, is a modern innovation. If you want to use it, go ahead, but I am more of a purist. Another thing to watch out for with "modernised" rune sets or books like Ralph Blum's is that they change the order of the runes, which is a modification that I am less relaxed about. The order of the rune-rows is a meaningful one, and changing the order is arbitrarily messing with that meaning. Also, the ancient Germans marked the full futhark as a spell on walls and other things, so they must have felt that its order had some special significance.

Layouts

Below I give some sample layouts for runic divination. Feel free to invent your own as well.

The Norns' layout: this a quick and comprehensive way of learning more about a problem. Reach into your bag and pull out three runes, laying them in a row. Rune 1: the past and any subconscious influences on the question. Rune 2: the situation as it stands right now, and what you consciously know about it. Rune 3: the results of your present actions or attitudes, for better or worse.

1   2   3

Sól's layout: a good general reading. Lay one rune in the centre to represent your question, then lay four runes at the cardinal points (north, east, south, west). Rune 1: (north) what needs to be given up or overcome; Rune 2: (east) new hope/insight; Rune 3: (south) best outcome; Rune 4: (west) unknown factors; and Rune 5: (centre) your question.

<pre>
        1
  4   5   2
        3
</pre>

Nine Worlds layout: this will give a general impression of what is happening in your psyche right now. Lay out nine runes in three groups of three, so that they look like a square, as shown below. Rune 1: Asgard - divine inspiration, the key to transcending it all. Rune 2: Midgard - your immediate situation. Rune 3: Hel - hidden aspects, subconscious factors. Rune 4: Alfheim - the best part of yourself. Rune 5: Jotunheim - that which works against you, Rune 6: Svartalfheim: shadow. Rune 7: Nifhelheim - what leaves you cold. Rune 8: Muspellheim - what angers you. Rune 9: Vanaheim - fertility, prosperity, sexual issues.

<pre>
  4   1   7
  5   2   8
  6   3   9
</pre>

Rune Magic

Another way to use the runes is for exploration of the otherworlds. Each rune is associated with a set of meanings that correspond to one element of the universe. By working with these you can align yourself to the universe, or to the elements that you choose.

Once you have made your runes, spend some time becoming familiar with them. Learn the letters and what they represent. Consider the relation between the shape and the sound. After you have done that, spend time each day meditating on one rune, its name and meaning, and developing your personal associations to it. Try to relate them to your personal experience.

Once you have become more attuned to the runes, you may wish to perform more active rune magic. One basic form is making bindrunes, which are groups of runes written as a sort of monogram so that their powers are combined. This is the sort of thing that requires experiment, and several of the books listed below will be helpful here.

****
Women's Runes
Freya Aswynn, *Leaves of Yggdrasil*, Aquarian. This book is an excellent guide to runes and their use. She gives a psychological dimension to the readings that I find useful. Her chapter on women's mysteries is also valuable.

Susan Gitlin-Emmer, *Lady of the Northern Light*, Crossing Press. This is a good introduction for anyone coming to the runes straight from goddess religion. It contains lots of material you will be familiar with already. The down side is her deep reluctance to credit male deities for anything.

Nigel Pennick, *The Basic Runes*, Nideck (see bibliography for address) This pamphlet gives female meanings for all the runes, relating them to various goddesses. It is a good source of information on the feminine side of runes.

Standard Runes

Kvedulf Gundarsson, *Teutonic Magic*, Llewellyn. Along with its companion volume, *Teutonic Religion*, this book is a good buy. He has many suggestions for working with the runes, and good definitions of the standard meanings.
Jan Fries, *Helrunar*. Fries gives a very individual look at the runes, with a chaos magic perspective. He is very encouraging to the novice, and his ideas on runic posture are intriguing.
Nigel Pennick, *Rune Magic*. This book is mostly about the magical use of runes, rather than their use in divination. Great if you need a spell to get your life in order.

Correspondences

Table of times and seasons

Sonnewende	New Moon	Midnight	North
Disting		Small Hours	North-East
Oestre	Waxing Moon	Dawn	East
Walpurgis		Morning	South-East
Litha	Full Moon	Noon	South
Hloaf-mass		Afternoon	South-West
Winter Finding	Waning Moon	Sunset	West
Ancestors		Evening	North-West

The runes and their meanings:

Rune-name	Translation	Goddess meaning	Conventional meaning
Feoh	cattle, fee	Freya	prosperity
Ur	aurochs	female might	primal energy
Thorn	thorn, giant	giantess	defence
As	god, mouth	goddess, prophecy	speech, wisdom
Raidho	wagon	sun-chariot	travel
Ken	torch, sore	hearth	illumination
Gyfu	gift	love	gift, love
Wynn	joy	------	happiness
Hagel	hail	------	blight
Nyd	need	Norns	need
Is	ice	Skadhi	stasis
Jera	harvest, year	Fulla	fufillment

159

Eoh	yew	shamanic travel	ventures
Peorth	dice-cup	womb	chance
Elhaz	sedge, swan	Valkyrie	protection
Sigel	sun	sun-goddess	victory
Tyr	Tyr, pole-star	cosmic order	justice
Berkana	birch	purification	birth
Ehwaz	horse	sun's horses	control
Mannaz	human	moon-god	relationships
Lagu	water, leek	fertility, Vanir	fluidity
Ing	Ingvi-Frey	womb	potency
Odal	enclosure	ancestors	inheritance
Dag	day, dawn	dawn-goddess	completion

Gythia

The country people thought Freyr was alive and so it seemed in some cases and they thought that he needed to sleep with his wife. This woman was beautiful and governed the sanctuary and the place and everything concerned with the god.[121]

As well as priests, called gothi, there was a category of priestesses called gythia. There are several of these listed in Icelandic histories, mostly of important families. There was a woman called Steinvör, who had a temple (höfuth-hof) and received dues from merchants. There was a Thruridr-gythia, and a Thorlaug-gythia in the *Landnamabok*, who were probably local officials who presided in the temples of their area.

While the gothi was expected to maintain a public temple and participate in the administration of his district, the role of the gythia in Iceland is less clear. In Christian times a widow who inherited the office had to sell it to a man, but this was probably because the priestly part of the job was eliminated by the new religion. The Steinvör mentioned above seems to have performed the religious part of the job, while her brother took care of the more mundane aspects. When a Christian merchant withheld temple dues from her, it was her brother who dealt with him.[122]

There does not seem to have been any overlap between the gythia and those who practised seithr or prophecy. The role of a temple official was to see that the right ceremonies were carried out, and do their work as local administrators, upholding the laws and keeping up the temple area. Since often these were the only people versed in law and custom, it is not surprising that they became the local authorities. While the women did not perhaps have any administrative power, they still had to tend to the temple and keep up the rites. This alone would have kept them from wandering around freelance the way that völvas and seithkonur did. Neither of these two had any part to play in the structure of the state, and the word gythia is never applied to them.

Bride of the god

There are many women listed in the *Landnamabok* and other sources who were priestesses. It seems that the deity they served was almost always Freyr. In Magnus Olsen's *Farms and Fanes of Ancient Norway*, he studied what information was available about gythur, and found that they were generally associated with Freyr. Either they were connected to a temple, or their family came from a place associated with the cult of either Freyr (Freyshof) or Njord (Tröndelagen, Namdalen, Hevne)

He also found priestesses of Freyr in Iceland, among them a woman called Thuridr, who had hofgythia for her surname. This indicated that she was a temple priestess. This seems to have been the usual family position, since her brother was Throdr Ossursson, who was called Freysgothi ("priest of Freyr"). Their descendants were called Freysgydlingar ("Freyr's priestlings").

The story of Gunnar Helmingr, who passed himself off as the god Freyr, contains lots of lore about the priestess of the god. Since the people apparently regarded the god as living a life much like their own, the priestess was considered his wife, a relation with sexual overtones. Like any wife, she looked after his property, in this case by running the temple and its property.

When winter came, the priestess, her attendants and the image of Freyr did a progress around the district, so that they could attend the feasts and ensure good crops for the local farmers. Gunnar, who had sought sanctuary in the temple, went with them. As they were crossing the mountains, a blizzard came up, and all the attendants were lost except Gunnar. He and the priestess continued on, but finally he was unable to get the horse to go any further, although the priestess told him that he was making Freyr angry. Finally the idol apparently leaped from the cart and wrestled with Gunnar, who managed to defeat the image. (This is put down to a sudden return to Christianity, which drove the "devil" from the idol.)

After that he convinced the priestess to let him impersonate the god, and dressed in his clothing and took his place in the cart. Soon the weather got better, and Gunnar passed himself off successfully. He forbade the old human sacrifices, and instead took gold and silver, and other valuables. He amazed the locals with his ability to walk and eat, as well as his persistence in coming through the storm. He did not speak, however, as they were feasted in various places. Luckily for him, there was a good summer, so that there seemed to be hope for the harvest. The priestess became pregnant, and this too was taken as a good sign. Eventually, however, some of Gunnar's family tracked him down and he returned home by stealth, to avoid the Swedes' wrath.

Part of the significance of this story lies in a sardonic comment King Olaf makes when he hears of the success of the new Freyr, that the most effective worship is the worship of living persons. It also tells us that the Swedes were used to thinking of Freyr as a living person, so they were not just being gullible when Gunnar took them in. (Of course, the good weather and refusal of human sacrifice probably helped with this; people don't quarrel with anything that works, and doesn't demand too much of them.)

The fact that the idol of Freyr was transported in a cart with a religious official of the opposite sex, and numerous attendants, reminds one of the cult of the goddess Nerthus. Other details of Freyr's worship were also similar to that of Nerthus. In Freyr's temples weapons were not allowed, and during Nerthus's progress all fighting was suspended, and weapons put away. Both were supposed to give fecundity to the soil and humans (Tacitus called Nerthus "Tellus Mater", the Roman earth-goddess.) The goddess' island had a sacred grove, as did Uppsala, the centre of Freyr's cult. It seems that the gythia and godhi were concerned with the cult of the Vanir, and thus fertility and peace, instead of the magical or warlike cults of Odin and Thor.

Godhur and the Goddesses

There are two incidents in the *Eddas* which some think may show a goddess being served by a male priest. The first of these is the story of Ottar, in the *Hyndlajoth*, where he seeks the help of Freya so that he can win a lawsuit. Freya shows favour to him, because, as she puts it,

> *He a high altar made me   of heaped stones -*
> *all glary have grown t   he gathered rocks -*
> *and reddened anew them   with neats' fresh blood;*
> *for ay believed Ottar   in the asynjur.*
> (Hollander).

This suggests that while Ottar may not have been her official priest, he was faithful in his devotions to Freya and the goddesses. The rocks alluded to in the quote would have become "glary" from the sacrifices burnt there.

The second is the story of Gefjon and King Gylfi. He promised her all the land she could plow in one day, and so she and her four giant sons went to work and removed the island of Zeeland from the rest of Sweden. The idea that Gylfi was a priest of Gefjon is not supported by anything in the story. He doesn't offer her the land because she is a goddess, but because she entertains him when she visits his kingdom. It is more an Odin-type story about how a deity wins something by trickery. While these stories, especially Ottar's, show men relating the goddesses in a way that show their power, it seems unlikely that they were priests of these deities.

Duties of a gythia

The main duty of a priestess seems to have been to offer the sacrifices at appropriate times and maintain the temple. The gythia or gothi was a state official as much as a religious figure. The Roman flamen was very similar to the gothi. In Iceland, there were thirty-six or thirty-nine chief temples, which were administered by a gothi each. He ran the temple, made the offerings and in return received the temple dues.

The *Krstinisaga* has a description of a pagan sacrifice, carried out by a woman. In it a bishop and a man called Thor-wald went to preach to some people in Iceland. They arrived during the All-thing, and stayed with a family in the area. The man of the house went to the All-thing, but the wife and son stayed home. Thor-wald preached there, but meanwhile the wife, Frid-gerd, and her son were sacrificing in the temple. Thor-wald recited these verses:

> *I walked with the halidom,*
> *no man listened to me,*
> *I got mockery from the priest's son,*
> *the sprinkler of the divining-rod,*
> *The old house-wife shrieked against me....*
> *The priestess [gythju], god lame her.*[123]

This seems like a rather odd verse, but it actually makes sense in the context of a sacrifice. The priestess would be offering the animal that was slain, and the boy with the rod would have been sprinkling the blood about with his twig or rod. The blood, being consecrated, was sprinkled on the people present and the altar. Since most gythiur were involved in the cult of Freyr, they would have probably offered a boar, which was the god's cult animal. Oxen were also offered to Freyr, probably in his role as the god of agriculture.

Goddesses as priestesses

A verse of the *Gylfaginning* is often interpreted to mean that there was a temple to the goddesses in Asgard. It says:

> *...this was the sanctuary that belonged to the*
> *goddesses, and it was very beautiful. This building is*
> *called Vingolf.*
> (Faulkes)

Turville-Petre says that this sanctuary (horgr) was a temple of wood, with a roof, although once the word meant the kind of pile of stones that Freya says Ottar built for her.[124]

What is not clear is whether this was intended for the worship of the goddesses, or for the goddesses to perform sacrifices in. Sturluson generally refers to it as a sort of heaven, where heroes and good people go, which is an obvious Christian overlay.

It is not impossible that the goddesses might have offered sacrifices. There are some indications that Freya was a priestess as well as a witch. The *Yngling Saga* calls her a priestess, a blot- gythia, meaning a priestess who offers sacrifices. After the death of the god-king Fro, she kept up the sacrifices and maintained the temple at Uppsala, since the other gods were dead. Freyr had seemingly begun the rites there, although these apparently included human sacrifice, which was practised at Uppsala. [125] Human sacrifice in this case was often a sacred capital punishment; the *Landnamabok* lists several men who were sentenced to be sacrificed by having their backs broken on rocks.[126]

In fact, the word gythia is used for both the goddesses and the priestesses, just as gothi derived from goth, and originally "the divine". Unfortunately, by the time records were kept, the office of sacrificer had become an essentially secular one. Like the flamen of Rome, all that was required was that the presider be ritually purified and know the rites. As a result, all we know of their duties is the external rules of sacrifice. If the priest/ess ever personated the god/dess for the faithful, it was not recorded.

****

Tacitus *The Germania*, trans. H. Mattingly & S.A. Handford, Penguin, London, 1970. Describes the cult of Nerthus.

Volva

*There was a woman called Heid, a witch with second
sight, so that with her uncanny knowledge she knew about
all things before they happened. She would go to feasts,
telling people about their destinies and forecasting the
weather for the coming winter.*[127]

The völva was essentially a seeress. These came in two
categories, the ones who could see the future through
innate talent, and those who needed the magic called
seithr to help them answer their clients' questions. The
main questions that they had to answer were about the
harvest, the welfare of farm animals, and whether the
questioner would marry. Like all forms of divination and
mediumship, it was essentially a passive process.
Whether through innate talent or through summoning up
the spirits to give information, the seeress merely saw the
future, without trying to control it.

The word völva is often derived from the words for "round
pole" or stick. This is because one of the völva's tools was
a staff. However, the word for staff, völr, is also used for
non-magical sticks, and the word stafr is just as likely to
refer to the magical staff. The word völva had an earlier
connection with the Indo-European root *uel and its
meaning of "circular motion" (which links it to the words
for staff) and also "sheltering or enclosing structure".[128] It
is related to the Greek *helix*, Old Indian words for cave
and covered, Latin *vulva* and *involucrum*, covering, and
the Middle Irish word for fence.[129]

Women and precognition

Foresight seems to have been a female prerogative. Ordinary women could have a vision or flash of psychic insight, as when foster-mothers touched men's weapons or armour to divine whether they would return from battle. Women also often dreamed true; many sagas such as the *Greenlandish Lay of Atli* show what happens when men disregard these warnings. Often the woman who sees the future is a relative of the person who suffers from not heeding them. Another category of woman who prophecies is the one described as "heathen".[130] Thorhild in the *Ljósvetninga saga* dresses in war gear and hews the sea with an axe before making her predictions, and is described as "of the old way of mind".

Historical volvas

Some of the Roman sources also mention women who could prophesy. These women were probably völvas. The Veleda mentioned by Tacitus foresaw the German victory over the Roman legions, which added to her incredible popularity among her people, whom Tacitus tells us saw her as a "divinity". She lived in a tower and wielded her political clout through intermediaries. Others included the seeress who spoke to Drusus in Latin and so intimidated him with her predictions that he abandoned his plans to cross the Elbe.[131] The emperor Domitian met another seeress, Ganna, and sent her back to Germany after he had honoured her. These women seem to have had a sound grasp of politics as well as prophetic ability.

Julius Caesar mentions groups of women who divined and prophesied. They were old, wore white robes and went barefoot. They ritually slaughtered prisoners over huge cauldrons and drew auguries from the way the blood flowed. He also says that they examined the victims' entrails, which sounds rather like the Roman practice of checking the vitals of animals given to the gods. Plutarch and Clement of Alexandria also mention women who divined omens from the movement of water.

Unlike the seithkonur and the gydhiur, their magic was respectable, and they continued to practice in Christian times. Gregory of Tours mentions many prophetic women in his chronicle, reflecting the desire for marvels in these works. One was the witch of Verdun, who found stolen property, and another was the pythoness of Tours, who foretold the death of Charibet to the exact time.

Why they were tolerated is an interesting question. It may be because the Bible also has many instances of people prophesying, and this might have legitimated the völva's activities. Most of these instances involve men, however, and the witch of Endor and the Biblical injunction against all wizards and soothsayers would have counted against these women. Saint's legends, on the other hand, and the legends of the Roman sibyls, which would have come north with the Christian missionaries, are clear examples of women seeing into the future without upsetting the Christian applecart. This, along with a strong cultural bias towards accepting magical abilities as normal, would have enabled a völva to keep practising her craft.

Volvas in the sagas

Erik the Red's Saga describes a völva called Thorbjorg in some detail. She attended feasts in the winter, and made various predictions while she was there. The main character, Thorkel, was the leading man of the district, so he invites her to prophesy for them: *A high-seat was made ready for her, and a cushion laid down, in which there must be hen's feathers.* The saga goes on to describe her appearance when she arrives:

...she was wearing a blue cloak, with straps which were set with stones right down to the hem; she had glass beads about her neck, and on her head a black lambskin hood lined inside with white catskin. She had a staff in her hand, with a knob on it; it was ornamented with brass and set around with stones just below the knob. Round her middle she wore a belt made of touchwood, and on it was a big skin pouch in which she kept those charms of hers that she needed for her magic. On her feet she had hairy calf-skin shoes with long thongs, and on the thong-ends big knobs of lateen. She had on her hands catskin gloves which were white inside and hairy.[132]

The references to catskin suggest that the völva was somehow associated with Freya, since the cat was her animal. It may also be that the cat, which is generally regarded as a magical animal, was thought to give anyone who wore its skin special powers.

Other völvas included Heidr, who was a Lapp, and is mentioned in both the *Landnamabok* and the *Vatnsdaela Saga*. In the latter, she is invited by Ingjald and his family to give prophecies at a feast. People approached her one at a time and questioned her, but two heroes refused to ask her anything. In true warrior fashion, they decline to know their fate before it happens. She also appears in *Örvar-Oddssaga*, in much the same story. This saga tells us that she had a band of fifteen each of girls and boys who travelled with her. Also, in the latter saga she got the last word, speaking a verse telling the young man not to bully her, and then predicting a rather dire fate. When the hero then struck her, she left, saying it was the first time a man had ever struck her.

Helga Kness shows that there is a pattern to the historical sagas that have völvas in them. The völva comes from the wilds (Iceland or Greenland, then the frontiers). She is an old woman who makes a prophecy, and is given gifts. She takes her place on a platform or high seat, and sings or chants spells. The observers are divided into those who believe her and those who don't. Often Christianity and its adherents are opposed to the völva and her power.[133]

Mythology and prophecy

Odin, despite being considered all-knowing, consulted völvas twice. The first occasion was in the lay *Baldrs draumar*, when Baldr had a dream of evil omen. Odin rode to Hel and called up a dead seeress to tell him what it means. He clearly used powerful magic, since she begged him repeatedly to let her finish, but he made her go on until he had the answers he wanted. It is from this that he knew that he must make Rind pregnant to get the hero who will avenge Baldr's death. However, the seeress got her own back when she realised he was Odin, and told him she would not answer him again until after Ragnarök.

He consulted another völva, called Heidi, which led to the prophecies that formed the *Völuspa* (What the Seeress Saw). The seeress described the Norse cosmology, and the mythological history from the beginning of the worlds through the destruction of the gods and cosmos. After, she predicted that another world would rise from the ashes, with the younger generation of deities to order it.

Clearly these women were meant to be given gifts for their prophecies, since the seeress in this case tells us,

Gave Ygg to her	*arm rings and gems*
for her seeress' sight	*and soothsaying:*
(the fates I fathom	*yet farther I see)*
see far and wide	*the worlds about.*
(Hollander)	

("Ygg" is one of Odin's names, so the high god himself paid her for her services.) Other examples from the various sagas suggest that the völvas were well-treated. Saxo Grammaticus records that one had her lap filled with gold by small boys.

Interestingly, Odin also credits one of the goddesses, Gefjon, with knowledge of örlog, or fate. This is especially interesting because nowhere else is Gefjon shown as prophetic. However, the idea that women could prophesy naturally means that she may very well have had some foresight. Certainly, it was a good point in her defence against Loki's abuse. Frigg, on the other hand, is famous for her foresight, and Odin asks her advice on several occasions. Just like the husbands in the sagas, he lives to regret it when he ignores her advice.

Another völva is Groa, who appears in the *Skaldskaparmal.* Thor got a whetstone stuck in his forehead while battling a giant, and went to her to have it removed. She began to charm it out with chants, but he distracted her by telling her that her husband would be home soon, and that one of his toes had been made into a constellation. She was so pleased that she forgot her spells and a chunk of the whetstone stayed in Thor's forehead.

The völvas in the *Eddas,* including the two mentioned above, often rise from the earth. The mother in *Grogaldr* is called out of the earth by her son, so that she can chant protective spells over him. The seeress in *Baldrs drauma* is called out of Hel by Odin, and Heidi, too, (in the *Völuspá*), says that she knew the earth, and the nine worlds. As Lotte Motz suggests, the seeresses may have been like the pythonesses of ancient Greece, whose connection with the chasm below them gave them power.[134] Völvas were often called on to prophesy about crops and marriage prospects, earthy concerns that suggest that their connection with the ground of being was common knowledge.

The earthy source of their powers may also be the reason why the word völva is close to words for spiral, cover, hole and cave. Turning into the earth, as many prophetesses did, the völva could gain access to wisdom that was not accessible to those who lived solely on the earth. Caves are often the sites of initiation, perhaps a death-rebirth experience, or else an incubation period, during which the potential seeress would seek for the chants that she could "ride" into a visionary state. Perhaps they were meant to trigger her ability to go within and find an answer to the questions people asked her.

The name of the volva

The Heidr who appeared in the *Völuspá* seems to have been a prototype of the völva for the Old Norse. The mortal seeress in *Örvar-Oddssaga* was also called Heidr, who also appeared in the Landnamabok. Her name has been interpreted as "*Bright One*" (Clunes Ross) or "*she who comes from the heath/heathendom or the wild zone*" (Kress). as the "*Bright One*" she is the reborn Gullveig, whom the Vanir may have sent to stir up the Æsir and cause a war. (More on this in Origins and under Freya in Goddesses).

As the heathen outsider, Heidr/Heith in the *Völuspà* is another of the women who bind fate in the story of the cosmos and the deities. First the Norns come from the outside to determine the fate of the worlds, then Gullveig challenges them and becomes Heidr, whom they cannot kill. This provokes the war of the Æsir and Vanir, which further binds the deities' destiny. Thus the Norns limit them in a cosmic manner, and introduce death and time, while the war started be Heidr fixes the cycle that brings about the death of the deities. If the main preoccupation of the Norse myths is circumventing the demands of destiny and death, then these figures who lay down its decrees, must indeed seem foreign and frightening. This would explain the reverence the völva was given, as opposed to the scorn that a seithkona could expect. Only the heroes challenged wyrd, and even they usually lost.

****

Seeress or Witch? The Image of Gender in Medieval Iceland and Northern Europe, by Katherine Morris (University Press of America) is an excellent work on witchcraft and foresight among the Northern Europeans. It looks especially at how ideas about women shaped ideas about witchcraft, from pagan times to the witch trials.

Seithr

Niord's daughter was Freya. She was a priestess and she first taught the Asaland people [Æsir] wizardry, which was in use with the Vanes. (Monsen/Smith)

Although discussions of seithr and shamanism focus on the god Odin and the powers he acquired by learning it, seithr was actually considered a women's art. Odin, as the above quote states, learned it from the goddess Freya. This chapter will look at the "female" element in seithr, and try to determine what sort of magical practice it was.

The word seithr is related to words meaning "to seethe" or "to boil".[135] This could relate to several things. It could mean that the witch used a cauldron or pot, using the fumes from whatever was in it to entrance herself or for scrying. It could be a description of the trance state itself. Jan de Vries relates it to the actual state, suggesting that the practitioner actually could feel him/herself heating up and seething with the energies invoked. (Shamans are sometimes required to radiate heat from their bodies. Among the Inuit of Labrador one of the tests for a would-be shaman is that s/he be able to survive exposure to the Arctic winter by keeping him/herself warm.)

The powers that seithr gave its practitioners were listed by Snorri Sturluson. He states that after Freya taught Odin, he: *"...knew much of man's fate and of the future, likewise how to bring people death, ill-luck or illness, or he took power and wit from them and gave it to others. But in promoting this sorcery, lack of manliness followed so much that men seemed not without shame in dealing in it; the priestesses therefore were taught this craft"*. (Monsen/ Smith) This actually supplies us with a lot of what we know about seithr. It gives the user supernatural powers, it is considered unmanly, and it was mainly a women's art (at least in theory). The powers of the seithr-worker are an interesting mix, both passive (foresight) and active (affecting the minds and luck of others).

Foresight

The divination by trance was always led by a woman, which fits with the high status given psychic women in Tacitus. The section on völvas covers prophetic women and their methods in some detail, but the fact that they overlapped with women who practised seithr is interesting. Clearly both the passive ability to see into the future and the more active forms of magic done by seithkonas were not seen as clearly separate.

Cursing

Like it or not, harming one's enemies was a real part of Germanic magic. In the *Laxedaela Saga* Kotkell, his wife and his sons work seithr while seated on a platform. They have been hired to harm Hrut, and so they sang spells until Hrut's son woke and went out of the house, towards the platform, and died. The fact that Odin could cause illness, ill-luck and death with his new abilities shows that it was not entirely benevolent.

H.R.E. Davidson thinks that the harmful aspects of seithr can be linked to the fearful "night-riders". These women could turn themselves into horses and "ride" a man to

177

death. A king of Sweden was supposedly killed this way by a seithlkona, who crushed him in her horse shape. In the *Eyrbyggja Saga*, a man dies after a witch rides him to death. When the English King Edgar's wife was slandered, the accusers said that she took the form of a horse with her magic, and ran with the horses, "*showing herself shamelessly to them*".[136] This may have been a false accusation, but the person who said it was no doubt drawing on known ideas about witches, so that the charges would stick.

Causing confusion

The ability to "cloud the minds of men" was a part of the witch's repertoire long before the Shadow came on the scene. A typical example is the episode in *Eyrbyggja Saga* when Katla hides her son from his pursuers by use of illusion. She makes them think that he is a spindle, which saves him temporarily. Skroppa hid herself and her step-daughters from the outlaw Hord by making him think they were a sow and two piglets.

A different kind of confusion resulted in *Vatnsdaela Saga* when Thordis gave Thorkell her staff, which he touched to his rival's cheek. His rival, Gudmund, then lost the court case against Thorkell because his memory failed him in court, and did not return until Thorkell touched him again with the staff.

Freya and seithr

Freya is rarely shown doing any magic, except in the *Hyndlajoth* and *Sörla tháttr*. The first shows her turning a man named Ottar into a boar, compelling Hyndla to tell him his lineage, and then giving him a potion so he will remember it. This tale in particular shows her using magic and outwitting opponents in the same way Odin often does. Hyndla is not friendly to Freya's protegé and Freya has to threaten her to get the information out of her, and then reverse a curse that Hyndla puts on Ottar:

Witch, I'll encircle you   *with flames*
and from these   *you won't escape.*[137]

(Note that cursing was one of the abilities of a seithkona.)

In the *Sörla tháttr* Freya was entrapped into causing a war between two kings, and had to raise the dead to keep it going for all time. We know that Loki calls her a witch in the *Lokasenna*, the poem in which he insults all the deities. He says:

Be silent, Freya!   *thou foulest witch,*
   And steeped full sore in sin;
In the arms of thy brother   *the bright gods caught thee*
   When Freya set her wind free.
(Bellows)

Both Bellows and Turville-Petre translate that word as "witch", while other authors, such as Hollander, prefer the word "whore". If Loki is implying that she is a seithkona, the linking of her magical powers and sexuality would make sense, since seithr uses both.

If Freya can be identified with the witch Gullveig, as Turville-Petre suggests, then she is a formidable goddess indeed. Turville-Petre developed this theory to explain how Freya got into Asgard, because while Freyr and Njordr go there in exchange for some Æsir, there is no explanation of why Freya is there. However, the story of the war between the gods tells us that a witch named Gullveig came to the Æsir. According to the story, they stabbed her with spears, and burned her three times, but could not kill her. After that:

Heith she was hight   *where to houses she came,*
the wise seeress   *and witchcraft plied-*
cast spells where she could   *spells on the mind:*
to wicked women   *she was welcome ever.*
(Hollander)

This last skill sounds like the sort of thing one would expect from a seithkona. Gullveig means Gold-Drunk, which sounds like a name for Freya, who was associated with wealth, and who slept with four dwarves for a gold or amber necklace. Both she and Heid were competent in magic, and both of them caused strife.

The only other magical thing that Freya had was her falcon cloak, which enabled whoever wore it to travel the worlds in bird form. Loki borrowed it to rescue Idunn from the giants. While we never see Freya using it, we know that she travelled about in search of her husband, and also went to the world of the dwarves, from whom she got her magic necklace. Her many names, like the by-names of Odin, suggest that she might also have wandered the worlds disguised.

Ergí anò male shame

The quote from the Heimskirngla at the beginning of the chapter says that seithr involved "shameful acts" or ergi. (This is generally defined as passive homosexuality, or else expertise in witchcraft. Both were felt to make women of the men who practised them.) Another way that we know that it was a loss of status for men is that Loki taunts Odin about its use:

But thou, say they,   on Sáms Isle once
    wovest spells like a witch:
in warlock's shape   through the world didst fare:
    were these womanish ways, ween.
(Hollander)

In the context of the poem, Loki and Odin are exchanging insults about behaving like women. (Loki once gave birth while in the form of a mare.) This seems to confirm that men were somehow feminised by using this magic.

In a society as masculine as the later Vikings were, with their emphasis on violence, raiding and revenge in the sagas, it would seem that masculinity becomes a major anxiety. The idea that a man would voluntarily "unman" himself by doing something women did disturbed them. (This anxiety was so strong that one could kill an effeminate man with no penalty, according to Icelandic law.) The same idea is expressed by Greek stories about Hercules spinning wool for Omphale, or Achilles living among the women. It may be that when the Norse led more peaceful lives, they were more relaxed about gender, but when various pressures brought about the Viking age, these roles seem to have rigidified.

Despite this, the sources tell us that both men and women did practice seithr, who were called seithhmenn and seithkonur. The men may have had to dress like women to practice this sort of magic, which in a society as anxious about unmanly men as the Norse, would have been shameful for the men. (An interesting book called *The Unmanly Man*, by Preben Meulengracht Sprenser, discusses the extent of the taboo on any sort of female behaviour for men. Women, on the other hand, could imitate men because this was seen as "moving up" the gender hierarchy.)

Clunies Ross has suggested that the reason that men were "feminised" by practising seithr was that they had to make themselves receptive to the spirits they worked with. Since a receptive position is considered a feminine one, this would make the men feminine, in the same way that being the receiver in a homosexual act would. (It is not just the Norse that see it that way, many people still classify homosexual acts that way.) The males who use it were generally disapproved of by their society, and morally condemned. That it was morally condemned goes without question. In the *Heimskringla,* when Rgnvaldr Rettilbeini becomes a seithmann, his father sends his half-brother Eirikr Bloodaxe against him. Eirikr then has his brother burned, along with eighty other seithmenn, which earned him great praise.

There was a female equivalent to ergi, called org. This implied lascivious or perverted behaviour. In the *Lokasenna* Loki accuses several goddesses of org, including Freya, Frigg and Gefjon (and possibly Skadhi, whom he says had sex with him). The female version doesn't seem to be linked to magic.

Women's magic

If men were feminised by doing seithr, it may have been because it was a women's preserve. A man performing a seithr ceremony may have been as incongruous as a man spinning or weaving. Sturluson tells us that priestesses were the experts who learned the craft. This implies that there was some sort of special training involved. We know that seeing the future was a feminine skill, to the extent that even ordinary women could have precognitive flashes.

Even in the mythical sources, Freya and Heidr/Gullveig are the only women who practised seithr. Odin did so, but he was condemned for it, since it involved a loss of masculine status. Clunies Ross suggests that the murder of Gullveig was the Æsir's way of telling the Vanir that they would have nothing to do with this women's sorcery. The fact that men were passive before the spirits would have been at the back of that rejection, since that would make women of them.

Almost all the human practitioners of seithr are women. The völvas are often viewed as being the remnants of pagan tradition, women who travel about using their powers of prophecy. Others were witches, like Katla and Skroppa, who used their powers for active magic. In *Fridthófs Saga* two women work magic on a platform, and are seen riding a whale some ways away, presumably sending their spirits or fetches to the whale. More benignly, a Norwegian seeress was able to use seithr to attract fish into the sound. The fact that most of the seithr-users are the last of their kind is not surprising, since most of our information comes from the conversion period.

Shamanism?

Most writers think that seithr was a kind of shamanism. I don't agree, and there are several reasons why I think so. First, because many writers misread the section of the *Yngling saga* that tells us what Odin's powers were. The whole section lists various things he could do, but only a few of them relate to the seithr he learned from Freya. The most shamanic sounding ones are not part of the seithr package, such as sending his soul forth as an animal while lying in a trance.

These skills probably became part of the Norse magician's repertoire via the Lapps. They were famous for their magic, to the point that whenever a saga wants to say that someone is powerful in magic, they say s/he learned it from the Lapps. The Lapps got many religious ideas from the Norse, including several deities, so there was certainly an exchange going on. The Lapps definitely used shamanism, along with most of the Finno-Ugric peoples.

However, the Lapps did not allow women to be shamans, at least in theory. According to Bäckman, there were women who were sorcerers, and a few minor shamans, but women could not achieve the top rank of shamanism.[138] Among other things, they were not allowed to touch drums. They even had to avoid the path by which the men carried the drum around.

One male shaman she mentions said that while his mother taught him his skills, he had to make a drum for himself. (The drum was the shaman's tool, without which s/he couldn't function. Other items of clothing and such went into a shaman's equipment, but the drum was indispensable.)

The skills that women were generally considered to have, on the other hand, were rather like those of the seithkona: they could foresee the future, cause illusions, injure or heal people, and alter the weather. These women were referred to as "sorceress" or "witch" in the early sources. (The word was Gåbeskid or Guaps while men were called Noide.[139]) They often possessed the evil eye, which seems to be connected with illusions.

Among the Saami, women were seers or keeners, who led the laments at all occasions of parting (weddings, conscriptions, funerals) and sang the dead soul to its new home.[140] This last skill in particular, could be associated with necromancy, which occurs in the saga of Hadingus. These skills, which are not shamanic, could easily have been passed to Norse seithkona.

With regards to seithr, it is noticeable that there are no accounts of anyone using a drum to do seithr, which was essential to Lapp and Finno-Ugrian shamanism. There was chanting, sometimes by a hired chorus, and the seithkona sometimes sat on a platform called a seithhjallr, and held a staff called a seithstafr. Also, in most of the accounts of people doing seithr, there is no mention of them being in a trance.

Dumézil quotes from *Vatnsdaelasaga*, in which both a völva and three Finns did magic. The völva sat in the hall, and argued with Ingimundr about her prediction that he would go to Iceland, and that he would find his amulet there. The Finns, on the other hand, went into a typical shamanic trance and did so in private.

Also, if any one of the deities was shamanic, it was Odin. None of Freya's exploits are particularly shamanic, although they fit well into a definition of witchcraft. She rode through the night on an animal, cursed Hyndla, deceived Hyndla's sight, confused the mind, and is closely associated with cats. Odin, however, underwent an initiatory ordeal, and learned the runes as a result. He also used to send his form through the worlds, and has animal "allies" in his two ravens, Hugin and Munin, who fly through the worlds to bring Odin news, and his two wolves.

Galòr and Seíthr: High and Low Magic

As mentioned above, Odin also practised magic. He was especially associated with the form of magic called galdr,

which involved chanting and songs. This form of magic
takes on a certain significance in this light:

> *All these crafts he taught with runes and songs*
> *which were called galdrar (enchantments) and so the*
> *Asa people were called galdra smiths.*
> (Monsen/Smith)

So the Æsir were the ones who used galdr, and this
passage from the *Heimskringla* continues by saying that
Odin also practised seithr, and defines it with the passage
quoted above. The two forms of magic were associated
with the two groups of gods, and have the same sort of
value that the Æsir and Vanir had.

When the war between the two groups ended, they
exchanged hostages, and Freya taught Odin seithr and
became his wife or mistress. Notice, however, that Odin
didn't teach her galdr, which would seem like the
reciprocal gesture. Just as with marriages, the Æsir
husbanded their powers while making use of other
groups' forms of power. The implication seems to be that
just as the Æsir were the top group, so their magic was
the approved magic. They disliked the Vanir's way of
arranging marriage (incestuously) and the Vanir magic is
condemned in the strongest possible terms. It therefore
became "low" magic, associated with a lower group than
the galdr magic of the leaders.

Seithr as witchcraft

The fact that seithr was a low magic, then, condemned it
to a sort of underground existence. While galdr seems to
have influenced the development of "high magic" or
Christian theurgy, seithr probably went into the stew that
made up medieval witchcraft. As I mentioned earlier, all

the abilities that went into the seithr practitioner's "toolkit" were the kind of things that we think of witches doing. Witches cast spells, using various verbal incantations or chants, they have commerce with spirits or demons (Greek and Babylonian magic), they can see the future or know intuitively why someone has come to them, they can cause harm to others, including causing mental confusion, illness and death. Odin, in this context, was not only crossing gender but also class boundaries. He moved from the more respected magic of galdr to the lower form called seithr.

****

Books to read:
Shamanism: Archaic Techniques of Ecstasy, Mircea Eliade, Arkana, 1988 (trans. William Trask) Love it or loathe it, this is the book on shamanism. Eliade takes evidence from around the globe to prove that shamanism is designed to arouse feelings of ecstasy in the practitioner. Lots to read and consider.
The Witch Figure, ed. Venetia Newall, Routledge and Kegan Paul, 1973.
H.R.E. Davidson's article "*Hostile Magic in the Icelandic Sagas*" is a very interesting discussion of the various types of magic employed in the sagas, mostly by women. She thinks seithr is shamanic and mostly hostile. (There are many other interesting articles in this book.)
Helrunar, Jan Fries, Mandrake Press, 199?. This is a very interesting take on the runes, shamanism and seithr-magic. He uses a very intuitive approach, which seems to stem from Chaos magic. I recommend it.

Demí-Goddesses

Nornír/Norns

The Norns are in some ways the most obvious part of Norse mythology, and also the most misunderstood. The main description of them occurs in the *Völupsá*:

Thence wise maidens   *three betake them-*
under spreading boughs   *their bower stands-*
[Urth is one hight,   *the other, Verthandi,*
Skuld the third: *they scores did cut,]*
they laws did make,   *they lives did choose:*
for the children of men   *they marked their fates.*
(Terry)

These names, Urht, Verthandi, and Skuld, have caused much controversy about their meaning. Urth probably means something like "fate" as it is used in the *Eddas*, and is the past tense of "to become", meaning something like "to come to pass". Verthandi indicates "being", the present tense.

Skuld is more interesting, since her name means "shall, must" and thus indicates debt or obligation rather than the future tense we might expect.

The idea of Skuld as future is misguided; she represented the working-out of what was set in place. Since no

Germanic language has a future tense (but must use auxiliary words to form the future) the simple idea of the Norns as past-present-future is invalid.

Tied to this idea of the Norns marking out all time is the idea of them as maiden-mother-crone. This is also unlikely, since all the references call them "maidens". The idea probably comes from the Greek Moriae and the Roman Parcae, who were shown as a young, middle-aged and old woman to symbolise the progression of time. In fact, the Norns are often subsumed into one, Urth. The Norse seem to have viewed her as the main Norn, perhaps because of their view of destiny as arising from the past.

The Norns are present at the beginning of time, and set the fate of the world. Apparently of giant origin, they appear to the gods, who are playing a game. While it does not say who they are, it is assumed that they are the Norns. It says: *"but there came three maidens monstrous to look at, giant daughters of Jotunheim."* (Terry) Later in the poem, as quoted above, they cast the runes and so determine what the world's fate will be. It seems, from the context, that until the Norns arrived, a sort of Golden Age existed, with no conflicts or death. After they came, the war between the Æsir and Vanir began, and the first conflict between Thor and the giants commenced.

The Norns also seem to be connected to the world-tree Yggdrasil. They lived under its branches, where they cut runes to mark out destiny. Urth's well was under one of the roots of the tree, and it is also said further that "*the Norns who live near the spring of Urth draw water from the spring every day, and along with it the clay that lies round the spring, and they besprinkle the ash so that its branches will not wither or decay*". (Young) Urth's well was also said to be a centre of Asgard, which made it a sort of axis mundi, which fits with its location under the cosmic tree. Urth's well is one of three, each of which is under one of Yggdrasil's three roots.

As well as the three main Norns, there were norns of various kinds, who looked after the different races of Norse myth. I quoted a passage from the *Fafnismál* which says that humans, elves and dwarves have their own norns. This corresponds with the idea of personal norns, who set one's destiny at birth. The passage quoted above goes on to say that good norns give a favourable destiny, while less kindly ones give a harsh life.

Another example of this is the story of Norna-Gest, which has an almost fairy-tale quality. When he was a baby, his father invited "spae-women" to the house to prophesy his son's destiny. Three women came, in the style of the völvas (large following, gifts given, hospitality extended) and went to the boy's cradle. The first two women said that Norna-Gest would have a lucky life, and he would be greater than all the other men in the area. The third woman, who felt slighted and had been pushed from her seat by some of the onlookers, said that he would live no longer than the nearby candle burned.

The eldest woman then rescued the situation by blowing out the candle, and giving it to his mother to keep. She told her to burn it only on the last day of his life. When Norna-Gest became a man, his mother gave it to him to keep.[141] These women who could see the future were probably völvas, and were called norns because they filled the same function as the Norns did for the gods. It is easy to see how having a völva foretell your child's future could become popular.

Another such incident was the story of how the Danish king Fridleif took his son Olaf to the temple, to pray to the "*three maidens sitting on three seats*". The first two gave him the gifts of charm and generosity, but the third decreed that he should be stingy in gift-giving. (This would be a problem for a king who essentially had to bribe his supporters into staying with him.) Whether this story refers to images in the temple, an apparition of the Norns, or three völvas who made a prophecy is not clear.

This idea that the Norns gave a child his or her destiny appeared at humbler levels as well. The German Penitential asked women: "*Hast thou, as certain women at certain times do, prepared a table in thy house, and placed food and drink with three knives, that if those sisters called by the ancients Parcae come, they are there refreshed, and dost thou believe that they are able now or in the future to benefit thee?*"[142] This ceremony was supposed to bribe the Norns into giving a child a good destiny.

The Norns were often mentioned in heroic sagas, where the idea of predestination was common. In *Gudrúnarhvot*, Gudrun says:

> "*I fled to the sea,*   *hating my fate,*
> *trying to defy*   *the Norns' decrees;*
> *I wanted to drown*   *but the high waves held me,*
> *led me to land*   *and I had to live.*
> (Terry)

In *Helgaqvida Hundingsbana onnor*, Helgi describes a battle:

> "*Sigrun, I will grieve you*   *by what I say*
> *but evil Norns*   *must bear the blame:*
> *there fell this morning*   *at Freka Stone*
> *Bragi and Hogni;*   *I was their bane.*"
> (Terry)

191

These few examples, picked out the many in heroic literature, just how important the concept of fate was for the Norse.

Fylgíur

The fylgia was a sort of fetch or double, who often shadowed the heroes in the sagas. These doubles, however, were women, while the heroes were obviously men. The name of these women seems to be an old one; no one origin can be given for it. The Old Norse word *fylgja* ("to accompany") is often mentioned, and it is apparently synonymous with the word for placenta. Turville- Petre also says that the words *fulga* (a coating of hay) and *folga* (skin, covering) and *fela* (to hide) are related ideas.[143] He prefers these to the idea of a caul or afterbirth, although a caul also hides, since it sometimes covers the baby as it is being born.

The afterbirth as a companion seems an obvious idea. In many cultures it is carefully treated, and buried near a tree, or eaten. Sometimes the tree it is buried under is then intimately related to the child, and their well-being becomes interdependent. Sometimes the afterbirth is tied around the infant's arm until it dries up and is no longer lifelike.

The fylgia was essentially family property. In *Hallfredar Saga*, the men saw a tall woman dressed in armour walking towards their ship, across the waves. Hallfredr, who was very ill, saw that she was his fylgjukona (fetch-woman) and told her that it was all over between them. She asked his brother Thorvaldr if he would accept her instead, but he refused. Then Hallfredr the younger said he would take her, and she vanished. His father then told Hallfredr the younger that he could have his father's sword should the old man die while they were at sea. In the *Volsung Saga*, Signy says her kinfylgia has warned her not to marry Siggeir. In the *Vatnsdaela Saga*, Thorstein has a dream that a woman "*who had attended him and his family*" warned him against leaving for a party. At the party was a sorceress who wanted to kill him. On the night of the actual party, the fylgia touches his eyes and causes an inflammation, which keeps him from going, and saves his life.[144]

Valkyríur

The common image of a Valkyrie is of a woman wearing close-fitting armour, metal breastplates and a horned helmet over her blonde braids. It would be more accurate to envision them as similar to the bloody goddesses of Ireland, Morrigan, Macha and Badb, who haunted battles and incited men to slaughter. Like them, they had both a fair and a horrific aspect.

One of the most haunting images of the Valkyries appears in *Njals Saga*, when they appeared on the battlefield, weaving a cloth on a loom formed of entrails with heads for loom-weights. The pattern was of gray spears and a crimson weft. As they wove, they chanted:

> *We weave, we weave the web of the spear,*
> *as on goes the standard of the brave.*
> *We shall not let him lose his life;*
> *the Valkyries have power to choose the slain...*
>
> *All is sinister, now to see,*
> *a cloud of blood moves over the sky,*
> *the air is red with the blood of men,*
> *as the battle-women chant their song.*[145]

This song was called the "*Spear-Lay*".

The grisly, warlike nature of the Valkyries is borne out by their names. Hildr, Hlokk, and Gudr are merely synonyms for battle, while Herfjötur ("Fetterer-of-an-Army") and Randgrid ("Shield-Destroyer") refer to the Valkyries' role as the choosers of the slain. While Odin and Freya could select which dead they want in their halls, the Valkyries decided who will fall in any given battle. This power is like that of the Norns, who decided individual destinies, and indeed one of the Valkyries named in the *Gylfaginning* was called Skuld.

The very appearance of the Valkyries was designed to frighten. In *Helgakvida Hundingsbana I*,

> *A light shone then   from Loga Fells:*
> *and out of that light   lightning flashed:*
> *(saw the matchless hero   the maidens riding)*
> *high and helmeted,   on Himin Meadows.*
> *Were their byrnies   blood-bespattered,*
> *from their spear points   bright sparks flew forth.*
> (Hollander)

In many heroic sagas one of the characters dreams of women with a trough of blood, or riding a wolf, which is the Valkyrie visiting him in his sleep. Like the Irish goddesses mentioned above, these women were often associated with ravens and other carrion birds. (Badb means crow, and the Morrigan was associated with ravens.) One of the earliest Norse poems, *Hrafnsmál*, is a dialogue between a Valkyrie and a raven. Both ravens and the Valkyries were associated with Odin, who was a battle-god.

The other aspect of the Valkyrie was a much more pleasant one. When they carried the mead-horns to the slain heroes in Valhalla, they were performing a more womanly task, and thus tended to be described as fair and pleasing. Depictions of this always show the women in typical female dress: a long robe, cloak, hair bound, jewellery. Obviously the women, no matter what they had done for the men in battle, had to go back to serving out the food and drink. They could also be swan-maidens, as in the *Volundarkvida*, which describes the women as Valkyries.

The Valkyrie could also be a personal tutor. In this aspect they were also called fair, white-armed, sun-bright. The group of poems about Helgi Hjorrarthsson show the influence of the Valkyrie on the hero. When a child, he saw nine Valkyries riding past a grave-mound, and one of them named and advised him. With her help he won a great sword for himself.

This woman, Svava, later helped him in battles, floating over his head in swan shape. Another Valkyrie, Sigrun, appeared in *Helgaqvida Hundingsbana in fyrri*, where she protects Helgi Hundingsbane. It may be that this Helgi and Sigrun are Helgi and Svava reborn, as *Helgaqvida Hjorvardzsonar* says they were. Both Svava and Sigrun used magic to help their chosen heroes, rather than fighting directly beside them.

A Valkyrie could also imbue a mortal maiden with supernatural powers. Brunhild was a mortal who was bound to Odin's service, and of course was punished after she awarded victory to the man Odin wanted to die. She wore armour, rode to battle, and was called a "Wish-maiden", but was still a mortal woman.

Sigrun was another human Valkyrie, the human daughter of the king Hogni, who eventually married Helgi. Many Valkyries were said to come from the south, including Sigrun, the "southern dis". This group tends to overlap with the personal tutor type, and so tend to be fair rather than frightening.

****

Mythology of All Races (MOAR), ed, Louis Gray, George G. Harrap & Co.,London, 1925, Vol. II, Eddic Religion, by John McCulloch. Lots of interesting articles, including much of what I used here.

Myth and Religion of the North, Gabriel Turville-Petre, Greenwood Press, Westport, Connecticut, 1964. A good chapter on disir, fylgia, and valkyries. He doesn't really discuss the Norns.

The Well and the Tree, Paul Bauschatz, University of Massachusetts Press, Amherst, 1982. Lots of information about the Norns and the Norse concept of fate.

RefereNces

1 Canute, quoted in Jones and Pennick, p. 157.
2 Mallory, p. 84.
3 Motz, 1993, p. 16.
4 Motz, 1988, pp. 456-7.
5 Davidson, 1964, pp. 26-8.
6 Mattingly & Handford, p. 109.
7 Polomé, p. 72.
8 Ibid.
9 Mattingly & Handford, pp. 134-5.
10 Polomé, p. 84.
11 Caesar, p. 71.
12 McBrien, p. 50.
13 Turville-Petre, p. 7.
14 Linsell, p. 110.
15 Polomé, p. 126.
16 Jones and Pennick, p. 148.
17 Jesch, p. 25.
18 Clunies Ross, 1991, p. 37.
19 Turville-Petre, p. 160.
20 Ibid, p. 189.
21 Branston, p. 126.
22 Fell, p. 29.
23 Strutynski, p. 365.
24 Hollander, p. 280, n. 10.
25 Mundal, p. 307.
26 Fell, p. 27.
27 Monsen/Smith, p. 8.
28 translation from Dexter-Robbins, p. 131.
29 Motz, 1993, p. 106.
30 Monsen/Smith, p. 8.
31 McCulloch, p. 250.
32 Grimm, p. 302.
33 Turville-Petrie, p. 178.
34 Ibid, pp. 178-9.
35 quoted in Näsström, 1992, p. 197.
36 Motz, 1993, p. 98.
37 Dexter-Robbins, p. 167.
38 Näsström, p. 198.
39 Turville-Petrie, p. 188.
40 Turville-Petre, p 165.
41 Lindow, p. 131.
42 Ibid, p. 132-3.
43 Clunies Ross, 1989, p. 5.

44 Turville-Petrie, p. 186.
45 Faulkes, p. 30.
46 Näsström, 1992, pp. 198-9.
47 Ibid, p. 199.
48 Näsström, 1995, p. 49, n. 79.
49 Ibid, p. 59.
50 Mundal, p. 307.
51 Motz, 1981, p. 129.
52 Monaghan, 1995, p. 118.
53 Eliade, p. 245.
54 as reviewed in Talking Stick, no. 22, 1996.
55 Nsäström, p 196.
56 Mandt, p. 125.
57 Motz, 1988, p. 456.
58 Motz, 1993, pp. 16-20.
59 Clunies Ross, 1981, p. 374.
60 Motz, 1984, p. 101.
61 Motz, 1984, p. 99.
62 Motz, 1993, p. 78.
63 Steinsland, p. 220.
64 Motz, 1981c, p. 504.
65 Turville-Petre, p. 231.
66 Motz, 1973-4, p. 95.
67 Monsen/Smith, p. 337.
68 quoted in Davidson, 1943, p. 111.
69 Davidson, 1943, p. 115.
70 Ency. Rel., Vol. IV, p. 520.
71 Motz, 1973-4, p. 93.
72 trans. by Jesch, p. 65.
73 Enright, pp. 170-203.
74 Fischer & Davidson, Vol. II, p. 88.
75 Ibid, Vol. I, p. 212.
76 Jesch, p. 111.
77 Ibid, p. 166
78 Ibid, p. 162.
79 quoted in Jesch, p. 162.
80 Sawyer, p. 195.
81 Byock, p. 80.
82 Fell, p. 131-6.
83 Sawyer, p. 211.
84 Ibid, p. 211.
85 Jochens, pp. 143-4.
86 Ibid, pp. 169-70.
87 Frank, p. 478.
88 Williams, p. 114.
89 Poetner, p. 88.
90 Frank, p. 479.
91 Sawyer, p. 192.
92 Ibid, p. 203.

198

93 Andersson, p. 240.
94 Magnusson and Pálsson, p. 101.
95 Morris, p. 78.
96 Ibid, p. 79.
97 Ibid, p. 81.
98 Motz, 1993, p. 122.
99 McCulloch, p. 245.
100 Turville-Petre, p. 221.
101 McCulloch, p. 244.
102 Turville-Petre, p. 240.
103 quoted in du Chaillu, Vol. I, p. 414.
104 Ström, p. 99.
105 Davidson, 1964, p. 112.
106 Grimm, p. 270.
107 Ibid, p. 270.
108 Ibid, p. 269.
109 Motz, 1993, p. 127
110 Ibid, p. 130.
111 MacCulloch, p. 177.
112 Motz, 1993, p. 128.
113 Ibid, p. 128.
114 Jones and Pennick, p. 153.
115 Gundarsson, p. 47.
116 Pennick, 1993, p. 9.
117 Ward, 1968, p. 39.
118 Thorsson, 1992, p. 130-1.
119 Gitlin-Emmer, p. 93.
120 Pennick, 1993, p. 14.
121 trans. and quoted by Nasstrom, 1995, p. 55.
122 Chadwick, 1900, p. 297.
123 quoted in Kress, p. 297.
124 Turville-Petre, p. 239.
125 Ibid, p. 173.
126 Ibid, p. 254.
127 Edwards and Pálsson, p. 4.
128 Motz, 1980, p. 200.
129 Ibid, pp. 200-1.
130 Morris, p. 41.
131 Ibid, p. 31.
132 Jones, 1961, p. 134.
133 Kness, p. 287.
134 Motz, 1980, p. 202.
135 Gundarsson, 1990, p. 212.
136 Davidson, 1964, p. 122.
137 translation from Motz, 1993, p. 100.
138 Bäckman, p. 84.
139 Ibid, p. 84.
140 Sikala, p. 335.
141 Kershaw, pp. 35-6.

142 quoted in McCulloch, pp. 244-5.
143 Turville-Petre, p. 228.
144 quoted in Davidson, 1964, p. 131.
145 quoted in ibid, p. 65.

Bibliography

Edda, Sturluson, Snorri, trans. Anthony Faulkes, David Campbell Ltd., Guernsey, 1987.

The Prose Edda of Snorri Sturluson, Jean I. Young, University of California Press, Los Angeles, 1966.

The Poetic Edda, trans. Lee Hollander, University of Texas, Austin, 1962.

Poems of the Poetic Edda, trans, Patricia Terry, University of Phildelpia Press, Philidelphia, U.S., 1990.

The Poetic Edda, Bellows, Henry Adams, Edwin Mellen Press, Lampeter, Wales, 1991.

Heimskringla, Sturluson, Snorri, ed. Erling Monsen, trans. with A.H. Smith, Dover, New York, 1990.

Saxo Grammaticus: the History of the Danes, trans. Peter Fischer, ed. H.E. Davidson, Rowman & Littlefield, Totowa, New Jersey, 1980.

Encyclopedia of Religion, (Ency. Rel.) ed. Mircea Eliade, MacMillan, New York, 1987.

Works Consulted

Andersson, Theodore M., "*The Literary Fortunes of Brynhild*", Islandica, Vol. XLIII, 1980, pp. 236-49.

Bäckman, Louise, "*Types of Shaman: Comparative Pespectives*", in *Studies in Lapp Shamanism*, eds. Louise Bäckman & Åke Hutkrantz, Almquist & Wiskell Int., Stockholm, 1978.

Branston, Brian, *The Lost Gods of England*, Constable and Co. Ltd., 3 The Lanchesters, 162 Fulham Place Rd, London W6 9ER, 1993.

Bucholz, Peter, "*Shamanism - the Testimony of Old Icelandic Literary Sources*", in *Medieval Scandinavia*, No. 4, 1971, pp. 7 - 20.

Byock, Jesse L., *Medieval Iceland: Society, Sagas, Power*, University of California Press, Berkeley and Los Angeles, 1988.

Chadwick, H. Munro, "*The Ancient Teutonic Priesthood*", in *Folk-Lore*, pp. 268-300, Vol. XI, 1900.

Clunies Ross, Margaret, "*An Interpretation of the Myth of Thorr's Encounter with Gerriødr and his daughters*", in Specvlvm Norroenvm, ed. Ursula Dronke, Odensee University Press, Norway, 1981, pp. 370-91.

Clunies Ross, Margaret, "*Pseudo-Procreation Myths in Old Norse: An Anthropological Approach*", in Social Approaches to Viking Studies, ed. Ross Samson, Cruithae Press, Glasgow, 1991, pp. 35-44.

Clunies Ross, Margaret, "*Why Skadhi Laughed*", in Maal og Minne 1989, pp. 1 - 14.

Clunies Ross, Margaret, *Prolonged Echoes: Old Norse Myths in Medieval Northern Society, Vol. 1*, Odensee University Press, 1994.

Davidson, H.R.E., *The Road to Hel*, Cambridge University Press, Cambridge, 1943.

Davidson, H.R.E. and Gelling, Peter, *The Sun Chariot*, Praeger, New York, 1969.

Davidson, H.R.E., *Gods and Myths of Northern Europe*, Penguin, London, 1964.

Dexter-Robbins, Miriam, *Whence the Goddesses: a Sourcebook*, Teachers College Press, New York, 1990.

du Chaillu, Paul B., *The Viking Age: the Early History, Manners and Customs of the Ancestors of the English-Speaking Nations*, AMS Press, New York, 1960.

Dumézil, George, *The Saga of Hadingus: From Myth to Fiction*, University of Chicago Press, 1973.

Edwards, Paul, and Pálsson, Hermann, *Arrow-Odd: a Medieval Novel*, New York University Press, New York, 1970.

Eliade, Mircea, *Patterns in Comparative Religion*, Sheed & Ward, London, 1958.

Enright, Michael J., "The Lady with a Mead-Cup, Frühmittelaltterliche Studien, no. 22, 1988, pp.170-203.

Fell, Christine, *Women in Anglo-Saxon England*, Indiana University Press, Bloomington, 1984.

Foote, Peter and Wilson, David M., *The Viking Achievement*, Sidgwick and Jackson, London, 1980.

Frank, Roberta, "*Marriage in Twelfth and Thirteenth Century Iceland*", Marriage in the Middle Ages, in Medieval and Renaissance Studies Vol. IV, 1973, pp. 473-84.

Gitlin-Emmer, Susan, *Lady of the Northern Light*, The Crossing Press, Freedom, CA, 95019, 1993.

Grimm, Jacob, *Teutonic Mythology*, trans. James Steven Stallybrass, W. Swan Sonnenschein & Allen, London, 1880.

Gundarsson, Kvedulf, *Teutonic Religion*, Llewellyn, St. Paul, Minnesota, 1993.

Gundarsson, Kvedulf, *Teutonic Magic*, Llewellyn, St. Paul, Minnesota, 1990.

Handford, S.A. (trans,) *The Conquest of Gaul by Julius Caesar*, Penguin, London, 1951.

Jesch, Judith, *Women in the Viking Age*, Boydell Press, Woodbridge, 1994.

Jochens, Jenny, "*Consent in Marriage: Old Norse Law, Literature, and Life*", in Scandinavian Studies no. 58, 1986, pp. 142-76.

Jones, Gwyn (trans.) *Eirik the Red and Other Sagas*, Penguin, London, 1961.

Jones, Prudence, and Pennick, Nigel, *A History of Pagan Europe*, Routledge and Kegan Paul, London, 1995.

Kershaw, Nora, *Stories and Ballads of the Far Past*, Cambridge University Press, Cambridge, 1921.

Kress, Helga, "*The Apocalypse of a Culture: Völuspá and the Myth of the Sources/Sorceress in Old Icelandic Culture*", Seventh Annual Saga Conference, ed. Teresa Pároli, Spoleto Presso la Serede del Centro Studi, 1990.

Lindow, John, "*Loki and Skadhi*', Snorrastefna, ed. Úlfar Bragason, Stofnun Sigurthar Nordals, Reyjavik, 1992, pp. 130 - 41.

Linsell, Tony, *Anglo-Saxon Runes*, Anglo-Saxon Books, Pinner, Middx, 1992.

MacCulloch, John, "*Eddic Mythology*", in *The Mythology of All Races, Vol. 3: Eddic and Celtic*, George G. Harrap & Co., London, 1925.

Magnusson, Magnus, and Pálsson, Hermann, *Njal's Saga*, Penguin, London, 1960.

Mallory, J. P., *In Search of the Indo-Europeans*, Thames and Hudson, London, 1992.

Mattingly, H. & Handford, S.A., *The Agricola and the Germanica*, Penguin, London, 1970.

McBrien, Richard, *Catholicism*, Harper and Row, San Franciso, 1981.

Metzner, Ralph, *The Well of Rememberance*, Shambhala, London, 1994.

Monaghan, Patricia, *O Mother Sun!*, The Crossing Press, Freedom, California, 1994.

Morris, Katherine, *Sorceress or Witch? The Image of Gender in Medieval Iceland and Northern Europe*, University Press of America, Lanham, Maryland, 1991.

Motz, Lotte, "*Of Elves and Dwaves*", ARV Nos. 29-30, 1973-4.

Motz, Lotte, "*Old Icelandic völva: A New Derivation*", Indogermanische Forshungen, vol. LXXXV, 1980, pp. 196-206.

Motz, Lotte, "*Gerdr*" in *Maal og Minne*, 1981a, nos. 3 & 4, pp. 124-133.

Motz, Lotte, "*Giantesses and their Names*", in *Frühmittelaltherliche Studien*, No. 15, 1981b, pp. 495 - 507.

Motz, Lotte, "*Giants and Giantesses*", in *Amsterdamer Beiträge Zur Älteren Germanistik*, no. 22, 1984, pp. 83-108.

Motz, Lotte, "*The Storm of Troll-Women*" in *Maal og Minne*, 1986, pp. 31 - 41.

Motz, Lotte, "*The Sacred Marriage - A Study in Norse Mythology*", in *Language and Culture: Studies in Honour of Edgar C. Polomé*, eds. M. A. Jazayery and W. Winter, Berlin, Mouton de Gruyter, 1988, pp. 449-59.

Motz, Lotte, *The Beauty and the Hag*, Philologica Germanica no. 15, Fassbinder, Vienna, 1993.

Mundal, Else, "*The Position of the Individual Gods and Goddessses in Various Types of Sources - With Special Reference to the Female Divinities*", in *Old Norse and Finnish Religions and Cultic Place-Names*, ed. Tore Ahlbäck, Donner Institute for Religion and Cultural History, Åbo, Finland, 1990, pp. 294-313.

Mundt, Gro, "*Searching for Female Dvinities in the Religious Manifestations of the Scandinavian Bronze Age*", in *Words and Objects: Towards a Dialogue Between Archeology and Religion*, ed. Gro Steinsland, Norwegian University Press, Oslo, 1992.

Näsström, Britt-Mari, "*The Goddesses in Gyfaginning*", in *Snorrastefna*, ed. Úlfar Bragason, Stofnun Sigurthar Nordals, Reykjavik, 1992.

Näsström, Britt-Mari, *Freyja: the Great Goddess of the North*, Almqvist & Wiksell, Stockholm, 1995.

Pennick, Nigel, *The Basic Runes*, Nideck, 142 Pheasant Rise, Bar Hill, Cambridge, England, CB5 8SD, 1993.

Poetner, Rudolph, *The Vikings*, trans. Sophie Wilkins, St. James' Press, London, 1971.

Polomé, Edgar, *Journal of Indo-European Studies*, Monograph no. 8, 433 13th St. NW, Suite 2, Washington, DC, 1986.

Rosedahl, Else, *The Vikings*, trans. Susan M. Margerson and Kirsten Williams, Allen Lane, Penguin, London, 1991.

Sawyer, Birgit and Peter, *Medieval Scandinavia: from Conversion to Reformation circa 800-1500*, University of Minnesota, Minneapolis, 1993.

Sikala, Anna-Leena, *"Finno-Ugric Religions: An Overview"*, trans. Susan Sinisalo, Ency. Rel.

Steinsland, Gro, *"Giants as Recipients of Cult in the Viking Age?"*, in *Words and Objects: Towards a Dialogue Between Archeology and Religion*, ed. Gro Steinsland, Norwegian University Press, Olso, 1992, p. 212-22.

Ström, *Folke, Diser, Nornir, Valkyrjor: Frukbarketshult och Sakrahlt lungardöme I Norden*, Almqvist and Wilksell, Stockholm, 1984.

Strutynski, Udo, *"Germanic Divinities in Weekday Names"*, Journal of Indo-European Studies, Vol. III, no. 4, 1975, pp. 363-84.

Thorsson, Edred, *Runelore*, Samuel Weiser, New York, 1992.

Turville-Petre, Gabriel, *Myth and Religion of the North*, Greenwood Press, Westport, Connecticut, 1964.

Ward, Donald, *The Divine Twins: An Indo-European Myth in Germanic Tradition*, Unversity of California Press, Berkeley, 1968.

Williams, Mary Wilhemine, *Social Scandinavia in the Viking Age*, MacMillian, New York, 1971.

Index

81, 86-87, 94-95, 102-103,
109, 133-134, 137-139,
143, 145-146, 157, 159,
164-167, 171, 174, 176,
178-180, 182-183, 185-
186, 194

FREE DETAILED CATALOGUE

A detailed illustrated catalogue is available on request, SAE or International Postal Coupon appreciated. Titles are available direct from Capall Bann, post free in the UK (cheque or PO with order) or from good bookshops and specialist outlets. Titles currently available include:

Animals, Mind Body Spirit & Folklore
Angels and Goddesses - Celtic Christianity & Paganism by Michael Howard
Arthur - The Legend Unveiled by C Johnson & E Lung
Auguries and Omens - The Magical Lore of Birds by Yvonne Aburrow
Book of the Veil The by Peter Paddon
Caer Sidhe - Celtic Astrology and Astronomy by Michael Bayley
Call of the Horned Piper by Nigel Jackson
Cats' Company by Ann Walker
Celtic Lore & Druidic Ritual by Rhiannon Ryall
Compleat Vampyre - The Vampyre Shaman: Werewolves & Witchery by Nigel Jackson
Crystal Clear - A Guide to Quartz Crystal by Jennifer Dent
Earth Dance - A Year of Pagan Rituals by Jan Brodie
Earth Harmony - Places of Power, Holiness and Healing by Nigel Pennick
Earth Magic by Margaret McArthur
Enchanted Forest - The Magical Lore of Trees by Yvonne Aburrow
Familiars - Animal Powers of Britain by Anna Franklin
Healing Homes by Jennifer Dent
Herbcraft - Shamanic & Ritual Use of Herbs by Susan Lavender & Anna Franklin
In Search of Herne the Hunter by Eric Fitch
Inner Space Workbook - Developing Counselling & Magical Skills Through the Tarot
Kecks, Keddles & Kesh by Michael Bayley
Living Tarot by Ann Walker
Magical Incenses and Perfumes by Jan Brodie
Magical Lore of Cats by Marion Davies
Magical Lore of Herbs by Marion Davies
Masks of Misrule - The Horned God & His Cult in Europe by Nigel Jackson
Mysteries of the Runes by Michael Howard
Oracle of Geomancy by Nigel Pennick
Patchwork of Magic by Julia Day
Pathworking - A Practical Book of Guided Meditations by Pete Jennings
Pickingill Papers - The Origins of Gardnerian Wicca by Michael Howard
Psychic Animals by Dennis Bardens
Psychic Self Defence - Real Solutions by Jan Brodie
Runic Astrology by Nigel Pennick
Sacred Animals by Gordon MacLellan
Sacred Grove - The Mysteries of the Forest by Yvonne Aburrow
Sacred Geometry by Nigel Pennick
Sacred Lore of Horses The by Marion Davies
Sacred Ring - Pagan Origins British Folk Festivals & Customs by Michael Howard
Seasonal Magic - Diary of a Village Witch by Paddy Slade
Secret Places of the Goddess by Philip Heselton
Talking to the Earth by Gordon Maclellan
Taming the Wolf - Full Moon Meditations by Steve Hounsome
The Goddess Year by Nigel Pennick & Helen Field
West Country Wicca by Rhiannon Ryall
Witches of Oz The by Matthew & Julia Phillips

Capall Bann is owned and run by people actively involved in many of the areas in which we publish. Our list is expanding rapidly so do contact us for details on the latest releases.

Capall Bann Publishing, Freshfields, Chieveley, Berks, RG20 8TF Tel 01635 46455